OUR CHILDREN ARE CHEATED

OUR CHILDREN
ARE CHEATED

The Crisis in American Education

BENJAMIN FINE

HENRY HOLT AND COMPANY · NEW YORK

TO MY CHILDREN
ELLEN, JILL, AND CARLA
WHO DESERVE THE BEST EDUCATION
THAT A DEMOCRACY CAN PROVIDE

I WANT to express my sincere appreciation to *The New York Times* for permission to reprint the material that originally appeared there in a series of twelve articles. I owe a special debt of gratitude to Mrs. Arthur Hays Sulzberger for the support and co-operation I received from her. It was Mrs. Sulzberger who suggested that the *Times* make a survey of what is taking place in education, so that democracy might be strengthened and our way of life preserved.

Also, I want to thank the hundreds of college presidents, school superintendents, educators, teachers, and parents who co-operated with me. Everywhere I received the unstinting co-operation of all; for that I am grateful. I am also grateful to the American Council on Education for permission to use certain materials from *Unfinished Business in American Education* by John K. Norton and Eugene S. Lawler.

I want to single out in particular the National Education Association for the splendid co-operation I received. The help from this organization, as well as from other educational groups, proved invaluable.

Finally, I want to express the debt of gratitude I owe to my wife, Lillian Rose Fine. She accompanied me on part of the nation-wide tour and proved exceedingly helpful. Her constructive suggestions, penetrating observations, and deep-rooted love of the teaching profession proved a lasting inspiration to me.

Contents

BECAUSE the public schools are a vital part of our democracy, it is essential that they be maintained at a high level of operation. Through the schools our future voters learn how to be intelligent citizens in a complicated society; they discover that responsibilities and duties are as important as privileges and rights.

One hundred and fifty years ago the United States might have prospered without free education for all. Then we were a simple, agrarian land, with comparatively easy decisions to make. But now, with the rapid strides in our scientific and technological development, with the undreamed-of media of mass communication at our command, with our world leadership at stake, with the Truman Doctrine extending our Monroe Doctrine, it is difficult to fulfill our role unless we are fully informed and deeply conscious of our obligations.

Only through an educated, intelligent electorate can we maintain a democratic system. When our schools close, the dictators will take over and democracy will perish. It is necessary for us to believe deeply, passionately, earnestly, in our free public school system. We will have to give our schools more than mere lip service. Our clarion call for better schools will have to ring loudly throughout the land, echoing and re-echoing in every city, town, village, and hamlet. No child, regardless of his geographic accident of birth, regardless of his economic status, regardless of color or creed, should be denied an opportunity for a full, free, and complete education.

Believing in the importance of maintaining the democratic

way of life, and recognizing that public school education is essential, *The New York Times* conducted a survey to discover what is taking place in education today. This was a genuine public service in the interests of our democracy. If the schools were not doing the job the way they should, then it was imperative that the facts be made known.

With that as a premise, the *Times* suggested that I make a nation-wide study of our public school system. I spent six months examining the schools of the country. My tour took me through most of the important cities, through half the states of the Union, and into scores of rural areas. I had no preconceived notions; I wanted to see, at first hand, whether democracy was utilizing its most important ally—the free public schools.

In my tour I talked to hundreds of educators, teachers, board of education members, civic leaders, parents, and ordinary laymen. I visited dozens of schools of every type and description, from one-room rural mountain schools with less than four children, to large metropolitan high schools of 5,000 children. I had but one objective: I was a reporter, seeking as impartial, as accurate, as unbiased a story as I could humanly get.

In many respects what I found was shocking. Many school systems have broken down; education faces a serious crisis. Hundreds of communities cannot get adequate teachers. I spoke to men and women who have no more right to be in the classroom than I have to pilot a super-passenger plane. In both cases the results are likely to be disastrous. In the case of the untrained pilot, the crashing plane is dramatic and easy to understand. In the case of the inadequately trained teacher, the effect, while equally serious, is delayed and not readily visible. We will suffer the consequences of our present neglect of education a generation hence.

My story of the nation's schools is not meant to discourage competent scholars from entering the teaching profession. Quite the contrary: I feel that given the facts, the nation will take the steps necessary to improve the public schools. And once conditions are remedied, I know that more of our best minds can be induced to accept teaching as a profession. Teaching should not be a haven for those who fail in other professions. It should not be the afterthought of those who flounder and can find nothing better at the moment.

Give the public the facts and they will act. Once the citizens of the United States know what has happened to our schools, they will respond with enthusiasm and vigor. Within recent months many communities have raised teachers' salaries, allocated more money for school supplies, and bought new textbooks and supplies. It is not indifference that has kept the school systems in such a precarious state—it is ignorance of actual conditions.

This story is told in that spirit. I have tried to be constructive, to give the facts without sugar-coating. It may be unpalatable medicine for some, but it is medicine that must be taken.

Our democracy is at stake. Good schools are necessary if we want our democratic way of life to flourish. It is my earnest hope that our free public schools will receive the support that they so richly deserve.

BENJAMIN FINE

May 12, 1947

AMERICA'S public school system is confronted with the most serious crisis in its history. An acute teacher shortage, lowered morale, inadequate supplies, and a loss of confidence have combined to weaken public education in this country. Poorly trained, incompetent and in some instances emotionally unstable men and women, without the slightest interest in education, have replaced worthy teachers who have left the profession.

Main bulwark of the democratic way of life, the schools have deteriorated alarmingly since Pearl Harbor. Teacher morale is at the lowest it has ever been. Teachers have gone out on strike in a score of cities and are threatening to strike in hundreds of communities in all parts of the land. In some instances, notably New York State, the lawmaking bodies have become so concerned that antistrike laws have been passed.

Public confidence in the schools has dropped sharply. As a result, parents are turning in increasing numbers to private, parochial, and religious schools in the hope of getting a decent education for their children. While the public schools have been going downhill, the private and independent schools have gained in stature. Many parents, the country over, are sending their children to nonpublic schools. They give this simple yet adequate reason: "The public school in our neighborhood does not offer my child a good education." It is plain that the parents, the public, the average American citizen, want good schools. They believe in education. But they are distressed at what has happened to the public schools and to education generally.

The war has severely damaged the nation's schools. School buildings are in need of repair. School supplies and equipment are lacking. Overcrowded classrooms have increased at an alarming rate. It is not uncommon to find forty, fifty, or sixty children packed together in classrooms designed to hold a maximum of thirty-five. They crowd two in a seat, they sit on the window sills or radiators, and they strain their eyes and crane their necks for a glimpse at the blackboard. Sometimes when replacements are unavailable one teacher has to take two classes. The teacher has to struggle along, as best she can, under a double load. Even in large cities such as Chicago, Boston, Philadelphia, or New York, the standards have been severely lowered.

Teachers are deserting the classrooms by the tens of thousands. The teaching profession has lost much of the ground it had won in the past half century. Coming at a time when large numbers of veterans are clamoring for an education, the breakdown in the schools is causing serious concern to educators and laymen alike. They recognize the dangers to the democratic way of life and even to their own economic security. Sometimes only vaguely or indistinctly, at other times more clearly, they can see a close correlation between good schools and higher social standards.

These conclusions have been reached on the basis of an extensive six-month survey of the postwar problems facing American education. To get a firsthand picture of existing conditions, I made a nation-wide tour that covered the principal cities from New York to San Francisco. I visited dozens of typical rural areas in all parts of the country. I spoke to thousands of teachers, and hundreds of school superintendents, board of education members, college presidents, informed educators, and thoughtful, civic-minded men and women.

Everywhere the story was the same. The war has hit the schools a disastrous blow from which they are still reeling.

While other segments of American life suffered during the war, most have now returned to their prewar levels. Some have gone far beyond. This has not happened in the case of the schools; they are in worse shape than during the war years. Even though our national income has gone to record heights, the schools are still starved.

A tremendous teacher shortage exists. The teaching profession no longer attracts the top young men and women of the community. They can get more money, easier working conditions, greater community respect and more freedom by working for the government, for private industry, or for the neighborhood grocer. They can get more money by driving a truck, collecting garbage, or serving as a bartender than they can by teaching. Everywhere teachers are regarded with pity or scorn; too often they are treated as second-class citizens.

On every hand evidence of this loss of respect for the teaching profession can be seen. It is perhaps best summed up by the comment of a nineteen-year-old junior at Clark University. Unlike most of her friends, Sylvia is preparing to be a teacher.

"My classmates think I'm crazy to go into teaching," she said. "They think something's wrong with me. But I like children, I like to work with youngsters—and I think I'll enjoy being a teacher."

An honor student at a mid-western university wanted to take up teaching as a life career but has since decided to become an engineer.

"My professors advised me to stay away from teaching," he explained frankly. "They said I was smart enough to do something worth while for a living."

That attitude is all too common. You encounter it everywhere. The best-qualified young men and women of the nation are not going into teaching. Figures in this area are almost startling. Twenty-five years ago 22 per cent of all college students were in teachers' colleges. Today only 7 per cent are training to be teachers. And the percentage is growing steadily smaller.

College presidents, deans of men and women, professors of education, distinguished scholars, and leading educators agree that teaching does not attract their best students. They express alarm and concern at this condition—but they concede that pious good wishes will not change it. The problem is deep and fraught with danger for children yet unborn.

"In the ten years that I have been at Harvard University," Professor Howard Mumford Jones comments, "I have yet to find a first-class person who was preparing himself to teach in the public school system."

The best minds of the community shun teaching. They regard it as a stopgap or as a refuge of last resort. Many feel as though they were committing social hara-kiri by becoming teachers. Although the alert parent seeks the best teachers for his children, he doesn't want his own son or daughter to enter the teaching profession.

"Do I want my son to become a teacher?" a mother repeated with a trace of scorn. "I should say not! I have much better plans for him. When he grows up I want him to amount to something in the world."

What is the result? The education received by young American citizens, the future voters of the land, does not meet present-day needs of society. Although we are living in an atomic age, our children are receiving a horse-and-buggy education. Many are denied that well-rounded schooling so necessary if sound decisions are to be made in a complex scientific and technological age. It is essential that social responsibility and citizenship be learned in school; otherwise our technological developments may be our undoing. Our destiny as a nation, dedicated to the ways of peace and international good will, may suffer. The present gap between social responsibility and scientific progress must be narrowed.

Many educators and public-minded laymen are alarmed at this situation. They recognize the dangerous implications involved. They know that if our democracy is to survive we must have an intelligent and informed electorate. Moreover, they are worried lest our public schools lose their grip on the American way of life and disappear as the great leveling force in our democracy. Probably more effectively than any single institution in this country, the public schools have kept the nation united, have kept democracy dynamic and vigorous. In those sections of the world, as well as those parts of our own country, where educational opportunities are inadequate, low economic levels exist together with an illiterate, misguided populace, ready to follow any man on horseback who has a demagogic tongue and a sack of promises. Where the public schools are free there is little danger of dictatorship.

Who is to blame for existing conditions in the United States? Why have the schools been allowed to deteriorate? No one individual, no one organization, no one segment of society is to blame. We are all to blame. Society is to blame for its neglect of so rich and important a supply of natural resources as its 30,000,000 children of school and college age.

There are many glaring shortcomings which, added together, have brought about the school crisis. Primarily, the salaries paid to teachers are too low to attract competent men and women into the profession. The average classroom teacher in this country receives $2,000 a year—or just about $40 a week. Can society expect to get good teachers for that price?

Throughout the United States children are suffering because of incompetent teachers. Nearly 6,000 schools have been closed because of the inability to secure instructors of any kind—good or bad. Seventy-five thousand children did not attend any school in 1947—their schools were closed. Two million others received inadequate education. From all indications, 1948 will be worse than 1947.

Educational standards have been lowered. The amount of training received by teachers entering the profession at present is less than it was before Pearl Harbor. The average teacher had a year's less training in 1947 than she had in 1939! Sixty thousand teachers in the United States have a high school education or less! In only fifteen states of the Union—less than one-third—is a college degree or its equivalent required of teachers. Ten states permit those with a high school diploma to teach.

But even these normally low requirements have been drastically reduced. At present 125,000 men and women are teaching on substandard, emergency licenses. Few of them have had any preparation whatsoever for their teaching jobs.

To add to the serious school breakdown, teachers are leaving the classrooms in droves. Since 1940 more than 350,000 have deserted the classrooms. For the most part these were the best prepared and most competent teachers. But they were able to get more money in government, industry, or business.

In addition to teachers' leaving the profession, there is much restlessness among those who remain. The teacher turnover now is twice what it was before the war. Twenty per cent of the teachers—or one out of every five—are new to their jobs every year. This makes for an extremely unstable school program. Many classrooms find the turnover rate appalling, with four, five, or six teachers coming and going within a single school year. Children cannot get sound training if their schooling is interrupted at such frequent intervals.

That the crisis in education will continue appears evident. United States Office of Education figures indicate that the school population is now on the upgrade. Having reached its low in 1945, it is beginning to reflect the increased birth rate of the war years. By 1950 the elementary schools will add another 2,000,000 children to their rolls. In the five years after Pearl Harbor, 13,000,000 babies were born in this country. In 1946, 1,550,000 children entered the first grade, as compared with 1,490,000 in the fall of 1945. This figure is going to grow substantially during the next few years. By 1949, the United States Office of Education estimates, 1,940,000 children will enter our public schools, or about 500,000 more than entered in 1945.

The implications are staggering. For the next five years we will have to add from 15,000 to 20,000 new teachers annually to the public schools. At the same time it will be necessary to replace the 125,000 emergency teachers. Within five years 400,000 teachers can be expected to leave the schools either because of retirement, death, resignation, or disgust. Here, then, is a problem of first magnitude. Within five years the country must produce 600,000 qualified teachers.

But from where will they come? Before the war 50,000 students were graduated annually from teachers' colleges or schools of education. A typical year found 37,000 graduating from teachers' colleges, 10,000 from teacher-training institutions, and another 5,500 from liberal arts colleges where they specialized in education courses.

At that rate it will take this country ten years to provide the 600,000 teachers that will be necessary by 1952! Actually, the shortage will continue to grow worse each year; it will become more and more difficult to get an adequate supply. The country will be forced to train teachers to meet current needs, and at the same time prepare enough to replace the inadequate teachers now on the job.

To make matters worse, fewer persons are going into teaching than ever before. Despite the available jobs, despite the appeals made by civic and patriotic groups, despite the recruitment now going on, the high school and college students are turning away from the teaching profession. You cannot get students to go into elementary school teaching. That area is effectively boycotted. It does not have the prestige nor does it offer as much money as the high school or college position. Superintendents everywhere are seeking teachers for the elementary grades. They are ready to employ anyone who can read a simple primer, or can write his name.

Most alarming, though, is the lowered morale that has hit the teachers. Gone is their patience and meekness, the two virtues—if such they can be called—that have stood them in good stead through the years. Following the lead of teachers at Norwalk, Connecticut, who closed the city schools for eight days to win their salary demands, teachers in many parts of the country have become belligerent in their request for better working conditions and more money.

In all previous school history there has never been an important teacher strike. A few smaller communities, notably in the mining districts of Pennsylvania, did cause school stoppages a quarter of a century ago. But no large city ever had to worry about its schools' being closed or its teachers' going on the picket line. We just took for granted that the teacher would always be present when the nine o'clock morning bell sounded.

That can no longer be taken for granted. At St. Paul, Minnesota, teachers closed the schools for more than a month. Buffalo, New York, teachers closed the schools for a week. A strike was narrowly averted at Dayton, Ohio. Strikes are still possible in many sections of the country.

Because of this unrest, the teachers' unions are reaping a golden harvest. Both the American Federation of Teachers (American Federation of Labor) and the Congress of Industrial Organizations union report unprecedented increases in membership. During 1946 the American Federation of Teachers had the greatest growth in its history, adding seventy-five new chapters. And if the crisis continues, it will undoubtedly make even more spectacular inroads into the teaching profession. The A. F. of T. union now boasts 50,000 members, a gain of 10,000 in two years.

The C.I.O. teachers' union, a newer and more militant body, is gaining rapidly, too. It claims to have 20,000 members, nearly a third of whom are in New York City. But the union is now sweeping beyond New York in a drive to organize the teachers of the country into labor-affiliated groups.

Yet the teachers are still a long way from being radical. The National Education Association, with a membership of 775,000, the largest professional school group in the United States, is opposed to teachers' going on strike. So, indeed, is the American Federation of Teachers. But both of these bodies insist that the lot of the teacher must be improved, so that he will not want to resort to strikes.

Despite the occasional charge that teachers are communistic or engage in subversive activities, my evidence indicates that the overwhelming majority of teachers are patriotic, conscientious American citizens. School leaders, principals, superintendents of schools, and education commissioners all report that subversive activity in the nation's schools is so small as to be negligible.

However, the fact remains that there is grave discontent which, unless checked, can turn into unwholesome channels. That would spell trouble for the American system of public education. Educators and laymen are seeking ways to get the best qualified young men and women of their communities to go into teaching. They know that democracy cannot continue indefinitely with a poorly educated, poorly prepared electorate. This problem goes beyond the teaching profession. It belongs to the public.

Inferior schooling this year will mean inferior citizens ten, fifteen, or twenty years from now. The ill effects of inadequate training will be cumulative. As a result of the lowered standards in the classroom, at least 5,000,000 children, or one out of every five attending our public elementary and high schools, are receiving an inferior education. In some communities this danger may not be visible. The schools are open as usual; the children leave home early in the morning and return in the late afternoon. From outward appearances normalcy has been restored.

Too often, however, the normalcy is deceptive. I found that frequently the school, operated on a makeshift, emergency basis, was failing miserably; it did not give the youngsters a decent education.

In another sense, the crisis has brought about serious repercussions that may have far-reaching effects. Too many teachers, their morale shattered, lack a sound philosophy of education.

They are primarily concerned with themselves, with the result that their perspective has been warped. To them teaching has become just a job, a means of earning a livelihood. Gone are the joys of serving society, of assuming responsibility for growing young minds. The pioneering spirit has gone out of teaching. Unless the schools implant the ideals of responsibility and duty within the students, our democratic society is endangered.

Fortunately, enough teachers remain on their posts who possess the spirit of service and who are convinced that teaching cannot be measured solely in terms of dollars. If the community rightly understands the part that schools play in preserving our ideals and traditions, it will not take advantage of this attitude. A pat on the back is not enough. Teachers want to become respected members of society—and at the same time get as much for their service as a truck driver gets for his, or perhaps a dogcatcher for his.

One serious danger faces the country as a result of the school breakdown. Hearing about the crisis in education, reading the sad tales related by teachers, many capable men and women may decide against going into teaching. Ultimately, a vicious cycle will be established. The students who constitute the future supply of our teachers will continue to keep out of the teaching profession, fearing that the schools have deteriorated. And because they stay away, the deterioration will continue at an even faster pace.

What is the answer? I believe that if the community, if society itself, can be made aware of how serious the school situation is, greater financial and moral support will be forthcoming. The public wants its schools to flourish. Education in this country has passed the experimental stage—it has become part of the warp and woof of our democracy. As soon as the schools receive greater public support, young men and women will be eager to train for the teaching profession. Only with public support can we hope to get the best minds of the country interested in teaching.

In the immediate years ahead it is necessary that we ensure the educational profession the same respect as is now accorded the engineering, medical, dental, or legal profession. That may not be an easy task. Yet it is a worthy one.

In a sense, the school breakdown falls into two important categories: the physical disintegration of the school plants and the deterioration of teacher morale. Both the plant and the teacher are necessary if children are not to be cheated. That is the problem that is faced by the citizens of this country. It is a problem that will demand herculean efforts from all of us during the next quarter century.

No matter how difficult it may be, it is a problem that needs to be solved. Here is one cause that does not need any propaganda or sales talk. The public schools are our greatest asset. Democracy cannot afford to neglect its schools. To do so would be to court disaster.

Every state in the Union suffers from a shortage of qualified teachers. Despite the end of World War II, the public school system is still unable to secure sufficient teachers to educate the millions of boys and girls attending our elementary and secondary schools.

Everywhere the story is the same: the supply of teachers is inadequate, and conditions are growing increasingly worse. In many instances school superintendents, desperate and at wit's end, have hired taxicab drivers, mechanics, telephone operators, or retired janitors to become teachers. As never before, all communities, both rural and urban, are scraping the bottom of the barrel.

In a sense, Peter is robbing Paul to keep the schools open. Cities of more than 500,000 reach down to the communities of 200,000. By paying more money, the former can secure teachers for their systems. The cities of 200,000, in turn, look to those with 100,000 population, and so it goes, until the small town has to knock on the door of the little rural hamlet. Many communities, especially the rural or poorer ones, have no one from whom to steal.

The teacher shortage is caused by a number of factors, not the least of which is low salaries. But money alone will not bring teachers back into the fold. Teachers object to the community restrictions that they face in many sections of the country, particularly in rural areas. They dislike to lead the lives of Grade-B citizens, always at the beck and call of the

town fathers. They are strongly opposed to the political interference that oftentimes keeps them at the mercy of the community. They want to be free political agents.

Even before the war many schools did not have enough
teachers. However, in some of the larger cities long waiting
lists of eligibles served as a backlog for the systems. Even
though their salaries were cut and other restrictions imposed
upon them, the teachers remained in the profession. Many
eligibles waited year after year, with no place to teach. New
York City, for example, had nearly 5,000 on the eligible lists.
There they remained for five, ten, and even fifteen years.
Chicago experienced a similar condition. Some drifted into
other jobs; the rest clung on, hoping to get placed so that they
could get regular appointments instead of eking out an existence on a day-to-day teaching basis.

Then came the war. Immediately the demand for help of all
kind, skilled and unskilled, zoomed sky-high. The teachers who
were still waiting for appointments found it unnecessary to
wait longer. They took jobs with the government, with business and industry, or in the military services at much higher
salaries than they could hope to earn in the classroom. Instead
of the "no vacancy" signs on their doors the schools put up
frantic calls for help.

Teachers soon found that they could make more in one week
in a factory than they could in a month at school. So they left
the classrooms and put on overalls. Thousands of others found
good office jobs with the government or in civil service. Never
before in our history has such an exodus of teachers taken place.

Their leaving created a vacuum that has been filled with
second-rate teachers. Or, in many instances the vacuum, defy-
ing the laws of physics, has not been filled. Rural towns and
large urban cities say quite frankly that they do not have
enough teachers to run their schools efficiently. Moreover, they
have no idea where they can get them. Whether in the North,
South, East, or West, the same story emerges: the schools are
understaffed. Although someone is usually found to take over

the classes, that "someone" may often be incompetent or emotionally unsuited to teach. Often the new teacher cannot meet even the minimum requirements of the state.

The cry for more teachers is so universal as to be almost commonplace. I talked with school superintendents and other top educational leaders in such representative cities as New York, Boston, Philadelphia, Providence, Chicago, Detroit, Denver, San Francisco, Oakland, Los Angeles, New Orleans, Baton Rouge, Atlanta, and Washington. I also visited scores of small towns and villages where I talked to leading county and district superintendents, principals, and teachers.

Almost without exception the educators and responsible officials said that their paramount problem was the inability to secure teachers. The shortage exists on both the elementary and secondary levels. Primarily, though, the greatest need for teachers is within the elementary grades. Superintendents just can't find enough experienced or even partially trained men and women to take jobs in the primary grades.

"We are now forced to appoint teachers who, under ordinary conditions, would not have been acceptable," Dr. John J. Desmond, state commissioner of education, Massachusetts, observes. "They do not come up to the standards of quality, personality, ability to render service, or the general educational background of our former teachers. It means that some marginal teachers are now being employed."

A similar complaint comes from other sections of the country. The repetition becomes a monotonous chant.

"We need more teachers," Dr. M. D. Collins, Georgia superintendent of schools, comments. "Some of the teachers we now employ just call the roll. They can't teach."

The superintendent of schools in San Francisco, California, finds that the teacher shortage, particularly on the elementary level, is his greatest administrative headache.

"It's just impossible to get the teachers we need," Dr. Curtis E. Warren, the San Francisco school head, adds. "We've had to go out to neighboring communities and states for our teachers, but even at that we are understaffed. We'll take anyone who wants to teach."

But the high schools are not out of the woods, either. Such subjects as physics, chemistry, mathematics, biology, and the vocational, agricultural, home economics, and technical courses are particularly hard hit. Often the high school simply discontinues offering work in these areas.

Because of the severe shortage, high schools are utilizing teachers for subjects in which they are not prepared. For example, Colorado, typical of other states, does not have enough qualified secondary schoolteachers available. The state is particularly lacking in science, mathematics, and commerce teachers. Out of the 8,000 schoolteachers in the state, 2,000, or 25 per cent, are teaching subjects for which they do not hold regular licenses.

"We have many complaints from students, especially veterans, saying that the teachers do not know their subjects," observes Dr. John C. Under, director of the Colorado secondary curriculum. "If you take an English teacher and give her a class in chemistry, you cannot expect too much from her. And that's what we are forced to do today."

School systems throughout the country report that they are compelled to employ high school teachers for all sorts of odd teaching jobs. All too often the teacher is able to keep only one jump ahead of the student. However, the students, and more particularly the mature veterans, resent this inferior brand of education and are loud in their protests. Too many of the recently appointed teachers, whether on the elementary or high school level, are incompetent or otherwise inadequately trained.

Sometimes the schools cannot get any teachers; then they simply close down. During 1946 nearly 6,000 schools were closed because of lack of teachers. Seventy-five thousand children did not get schooling of any kind. For them the democratic concept of free education had little meaning.

All states report that they have vacancies they cannot fill.

Sometimes they have to transport children many miles to get them to school. In other instances the children do not go to school at all. In 1946 Arizona had 650 unfilled positions and vacancies; North Carolina had 858; Maine had 1,295. Mississippi, in addition to 1,725 teachers on substandard licenses, had 1,292 teacher vacancies. Oklahoma needed 2,190 teachers; Washington could use 1,000 more, Wyoming 400. Kansas and Indiana both had 1,000 vacancies, while Kentucky listed 960. In all, there were 70,000 unfilled positions and vacancies in the schools of the nation during 1946-47. The teacher shortage reaches into every state, almost into every town, village, and hamlet.

Probably Arkansas, with 1,000 vacancies and 2,800 teachers on substandard and emergency licenses, showed the effect of the shortage in the most acute form of any state. For Arkansas reported that 14 per cent of its children, or 45,000, were unable to go to any school during 1946-47. Because of the shortage of teachers, 225 schools had to be closed.

Superintendents in all parts of the country are advertising for teachers. Philadelphia needs 700. Chicago cannot find substitutes to replace teachers who are absent. As a result, sometimes high school girls have to take over the classes. The rural communities are ready to sign up anyone who is able to call the roll and come to class.

"We no longer ask whether an applicant can read or write," a state commissioner said with more than a trace of irony. "If she looks as though she is able to breathe, we will take her."

School after school throughout the country repeats the same story. Name any state at random—Massachusetts, Maine, Illinois, Ohio, Utah, Louisiana, California, North Carolina, Washington, Oregon—and you will find an acute teacher shortage. The hoped-for postwar improvement has not taken place, and this shortage has worked havoc with the schools. Sometimes the damage is intangible; at other times it is tangible. Yet the harm, whether tangible or intangible, is real and lasting.

"Although the children are not walking the street, it would be far better if many schools closed their doors," Dr. Benjamin W. Frazier, senior specialist in teacher training at the United States Office of Education, comments. "Then at least the community would know the serious nature of their problem."

Significantly, Dr. Frazier adds: "The teacher shortage, acute as it is today, will grow worse during the next five years. At present the big cities are living off the flesh and blood of the small rural schools. We will need a ten years' supply of teachers in the next four years. But we won't be able to get them. It looks as though we will never catch up with the demand."

In normal times the schools need about 90,000 new teachers each year—which represents a 10 per cent replacement of the entire teaching force, because of death, resignation, retirement, and various other reasons. Today the teachers' colleges are not attracting a sufficient number of students to meet the replacement needs. Moreover, the increased birth rate, with the imminent jump in the school rolls, makes the demand for additional teachers greater than it was in recent years. All told, the country can be expected to prepare not more than 35,000 to 40,000 qualified teachers a year during the next decade. Yet the best estimates indicate that we will need at least 120,000 new teachers annually. With less than half that number being trained, the teacher shortage, far from getting better in the immediate years ahead, will actually get worse.

Alarmed at this crisis, the United States Office of Education has set up a Citizens Federal Committee on Education to study the problem and determine what might be done to remedy it.

"The present crisis affecting the teaching profession throughout the country is of such gravity as to threaten the future of the American way of life," warns Thomas C. Boushall, chairman of the committee, who is also chairman of the Chamber of Commerce Committee on Education.

His warning is echoed by distinguished educators and laymen throughout the United States. The public, although still unaware of the gravity of the problem, is gradually becoming concerned with the plight of the schools. A commission, established by President Harry S. Truman, has made a far-reaching survey of the nation's school crisis. The Advertising Council of New York, in co-operation with leading school groups, has embarked on a nation-wide campaign to raise the prestige of the teaching profession.

Almost all of the states find that teaching is an unwanted profession. Whereas a generation ago it was considered a mark of high respectability and some prestige to be a teacher, today the teacher's post is scorned.

"We are in the midst of a first-rate teacher crisis," Dr. John K. Norton, Teachers College, Columbia University, comments.

To this Dr. Ralph McDonald, executive secretary of the National Education Association's department of higher education, adds:

"To say that American education is facing a crisis is an understatement. The teacher shortage has gripped every state with unprecedented intensity. Our schools, as a result, are rapidly disintegrating."

School systems turn in vain to the teacher-training institutes for help in filling vacancies. Typical of conditions found elsewhere is this comment by Dr. Arthur Linden, placement director of Teachers College, Columbia University:

"Of the requests that were made to us for teachers over the past two years we've been unable to help in 40 to 50 per cent of the cases. We have practically no people in the teaching field at present training for the elementary or primary level."

Educators complain that young people are not convinced that teaching can be an exciting job. As a result, the students turn to other professions, side-stepping education; and millions of children are receiving an inferior education, cheated of their rightful heritage, denied an adequate preparation for American citizenship.

"Such a situation would be bad at any time; to deprive children of good teaching is always bad," the Council on Co-operation in Teacher Education asserts. "But in such times as ours the situation is especially serious. As a people we face unprecedented national and international problems. Never in history have we so needed to mobilize all our powers. If we are to hold our place in the world and play our proper part in creating a better world, we must develop all of our intellectual and moral resources, we must give our children a better education than ever before. We cannot do this with teachers of substandard grade.

"The crisis in teaching is, then, a crisis in American life. It is not just a problem for the educational profession: it should deeply concern all of the people of the United States. All should understand the severity of the crisis and what it means for children and adults alike. All should know why the crisis arose and why it continues. All should understand what must be done to save the situation. Then all must act."

Reports from various sections of the nation indicate that the action is slow and scattered. The teacher shortage will not be ended overnight. If all the students now attending teacher-training colleges in Florida were to go into teaching, the total would be less than 10 per cent of the needs, for the next four or five years, of that state. The District of Columbia needs 300 teachers. The 1947 graduating class of the District's teachers' college contained thirty students; of this number only ten indicated that they expected to teach.

Since 1942 the public schools in Chattanooga, Tennessee, have lost 305 teachers through resignation and retirement, or 41 per cent of the total teaching personnel. Employment of substitutes often results in continuous changes throughout the year; a single class may have as many as six to ten teachers. Within a two-month period—from September to November, 1946—one group of fifth-grade pupils had six changes—five substitutes and a regular teacher.

Chattanooga, in common with other communities, recognizes that the prospect of filling existing vacancies or those that will arise in the future is discouraging. The University of Chattanooga graduating classes have, in the past, been the city

schools' best source of teacher supply. In 1946 only five graduates from the university planned to take up teaching as a
profession. Out of the five, not one applied for a teaching
position in the Chattanooga schools. Moreover, only two of
the high school graduates of the entire city entered teacher-
training courses.

"Unless something is done to attract more teachers to the
Chattanooga schools and to the teaching profession generally,
especially in view of the population bulge caused by wartime
babies, one hesitates to contemplate the conditions which we
will face in the future," the Chattanooga officials warn.

An extensive study made in California by Dr. Paul R. Hanna
of Stanford University predicts that a serious shortage of elementary teachers will exist until the middle or end of the
1950's. The estimate ranges from a 3,000 to 10,000 teacher
shortage annually for the next ten years. Since California had
12,000 emergency teachers in 1947 the shortage will continue
in intensity. The state will be called upon to provide more
teachers and at the same time reduce the number of teachers
who now serve on emergency certificates.

In light of the estimated shortage of elementary teachers,
the California report recommends that an extensive campaign
be initiated to attract a larger number of the more capable
young people into the teaching profession. This effort, it was
urged, should begin while the youth are still in high schools,
and the advantages of teaching as a life career should be introduced in pupil-guidance conferences and in vocational-guid-
ance classes. If this were done the state might be able to meet
its needs more adequately than it now appears likely to do.

Similarly, the above-average state of Ohio reports a serious
teacher shortage, far more acute than at any time during the
war. The rural schools of Ohio had 1,532 vacancies in the fall
of 1946; together with the vacancies in the cities this brought
the total to 2,031 for the state. College graduates who were
qualified to teach refused to accept positions—they received
more lucrative employment elsewhere. Young people do not

want to become teachers—the number now preparing to teach in Ohio will supply less than 10 per cent of the total demand for the state!

Evidently the wartime shortage of teachers, coupled with the sharp drop in the number who are entering the teachers' colleges, is beginning to have its calamitous effect. Superintendents, taking the long-range point of view, are extremely pessimistic. They cannot see any improvement until the community understands the importance of providing adequate support for education.

"The ascendancy of the United States in world affairs has not been accidental," the National Education Association points out. "Ours was the first large nation to establish a democratic educational system open to all through the elementary, secondary, and, in some measure, higher educational institutions.

"By virtue of public education we became a mighty citadel of economic, social, political, and even military strength. Our rise to world leadership was made easy by the fact that other large nations lagged far behind us in their educational efforts. Today the situation is being reversed."

Without a strong educational system it is difficult to see how the United States can retain its world leadership. Yet little is being done to provide the country with a sound school system. This is indicative of what we face: during 1945 the placement office of the University of Arkansas College of Education received 861 requests for teachers and school administrators. But—the total number of students who had registered with the bureau for such appointments was thirty-two! Noting that this condition is not surprising, H. G. Holtz, director of the placement office, comments:

"The attitude 'it just doesn't pay to teach school any more,' has become quite general over the country. It is the chief reason college students give for not taking courses in teacher education."

Despite the present attitude toward teaching, education is

by far the largest of our professions. In 1939-40 there were 1,170,593 men and women engaged in the profession of teaching, on all levels, including college. This is three times the number of doctors, lawyers, and clergymen combined! Approximately 90,000 teachers are required annually, in normal times, as replacements.

"Our public school system needs 160,000 new teachers to keep operating efficiently," Mrs. Pearl A. Wanamaker, president of the National Education Association and superintendent of instruction for the state of Washington, points out. "This is not an expansion program. It is a bare subsistence program. Where are we going to get these teachers? We won't get them until we offer them the same attractive wages and working conditions that other positions offer."

America faces a serious teacher shortage, far more acute than is commonly realized. A number of rural areas are without schools; students from urban schools suffer because of poorly trained teachers, or are sometimes sent home because no teacher is available.

For the next decade millions of children will get cheated. They will not get the kind of schooling that they are entitled to receive. The United States will lose much in the way of potential ability and natural resources.

Before we can lead the world we must prepare the minds of our youth to understand and appreciate international problems. Unless we have strong, sound, dynamic schools, our training will be inadequate. It is essential that this country provide its public schools with an adequate supply of competent instructors.

3. Substandard Teachers

AMERICA'S schools employ 125,000 teachers on emergency or substandard licenses. One out of every seven teachers in this country cannot meet even the minimum requirements of his state! At the rate we are going, half of the children of the United States may be taught by substandard teachers in ten years.

Before the outbreak of World War II, only 2,300 teachers, or one out of every 400, held substandard certificates. Although not all the teachers on substandard or emergency licenses are incompetent—many are doing an excellent job—yet the barriers have been let down. The way has been opened for poorly trained teachers to enter the classroom. And for the most part they are inferior.

What is meant by a substandard certificate? Each state has established its own certification requirements for its teachers. They range all the way from a master's degree in New York State to a high school diploma in Kansas. When the state finds that it cannot get a teacher who meets its requirements, it waives the existing standards by declaring that an emergency exists. Hence, the term "emergency" certificate. In most instances they are granted only for one year, on a renewable basis. Here is the way the number of emergency licenses has grown since the beginning of World War II:

1940-41	2,300 emergency certificates
1941-42	4,655 " "

23

1942-43	....	38,385	"	"
1943-44	....	69,423	"	"
1944-45	....	78,665	"	"
1945-46	....	108,932	"	"
1946-47	....	123,492	"	"

The growth has been discouragingly consistent. There has been a steady rise, with the greatest increase coming after the end of the war. The question of emergency certificates plagues every state, almost every town and village in the nation. Everywhere school superintendents and principals have been forced to employ teachers who would have been rejected under prewar standards.

In some states 30 per cent or more of the teachers are on emergency licenses. Washington, for example, with 5,754 of its 13,353 teachers, or 43 per cent, heads the list, and illustrates the extent to which emergency licenses have been granted. So do Alabama, with 6,989 substandard teachers, or 34 per cent, and North Dakota, with 2,323, also 34 per cent.

Not only the so-called poorer states are in need of emergency teachers. California has 23.5 per cent of its staff on emergency certificates; Michigan and Ohio have 15.5 per cent; Oregon has 29.8 per cent, and Virginia 19 per cent. Every state is licensing teachers who do not meet the state's minimum standards.

That the emergency licenses are bringing poorer teachers into the school systems is apparent. The facts are too glaring to be overlooked. Eighty thousand of the emergency teachers, or almost two-thirds of the total, have had less than two years of college training. More disturbing still is the disclosure that 36,183, or nearly one-third, of all substandard teachers employed have not gone beyond high school. Many have not completed their secondary schooling.

As a group, the emergency teachers are one year short of the regular minimum requirements of their state. Although there are exceptions, a majority of the substandard licenses go to immature young people, to teachers who long ago reached their retirement age, and to persons without any professional training. They are hired in a desperate last resort to keep the schools from closing.

As a result of this indiscriminate employment of teachers, the professional standards of the nation have been lowered. The average public school teacher in 1946-47 has gone to college one year less than the teacher of 1939-40. The number of teachers without a college education of any kind has doubled in less than five years!

In the United States at present we find this situation:

  61,191 teachers have not gone beyond high school
101,698 teachers have had one year of college
198,224 teachers have gone to college two years
  96,527 teachers have had three years of college
290,442 teachers have had four years
113,764 teachers have more than four years

Less than half the teachers in the country—404,206 out of 861,845—have completed a college education! Nearly 40 per cent, or 361,113, have not gone beyond the sophomore year in college. The number of teachers who do not have a college degree who are now teaching has increased substantially since 1940.

A special commission on teacher education and professional standards, established in 1946 by the National Education Association, is attempting to raise the educational standards of the nation's teachers. Headed by Dean W. E. Peik of the University of Minnesota's school of education, the commission has established a long-range program for the improvement of teachers. Thoroughly opposed to the licensing of substandard teachers, it would not permit anyone who does not have at least a college education to teach. The 125,000 substandard teachers are of particular concern to the committee.

"Would you go out and license 125,000 midwives or 125,000 taxicab drivers to practice medicine?" the educators inquire.

"Even though we had a shortage of doctors during the war, we did not lower the standards for the men who practiced medicine. Why should we countenance this in the case of teachers?"

The commission is now engaged on a campaign to improve the professional standards of the teaching profession. It plans its activities along these three broad areas:

1. To encourage outstanding young men and young women to choose teaching as a career.
2. To eliminate from teaching and from teacher education those who are not qualified.
3. To further the conditions necessary to attract and hold the highest type of teachers in the public schools.

Campaigns took place in thousands of local communities in every state. Teachers' organizations initiated the program, but the campaign itself was a community-wide activity, sponsored and carried on by citizens' committees representing civic clubs, business and labor groups, women's organizations, farm and religious leaders, as well as boards of education and parent-teacher organizations.

In turning the energies of the teaching profession and citizens' groups to the problem of teacher selection, the National Commission is seeking to raise standards of admission and training to the high level which is necessary if the public schools of the United States are to meet the complex needs of the modern world. The commission insists on these two goals: only persons having at least four years of college education, with thorough professional preparation, should be permitted to teach; only those high school and college students who are among the upper one-third in personality, ability, character, and scholarship should be permitted to enter teachers' colleges or teacher-training institutions.

Through this campaign, and similar ones that are receiving nation-wide sponsorship, the educators hope to stem the tide of emergency teachers that threatens to wash away all existing educational standards. Everywhere the effect of the lowered standards is evident. It is a wonder that the communities would not rather close their schools completely than permit incompetent men and women to teach.

In a town in the Middle West, twenty miles from a large city, I visited a small, three-room rural school, containing 103 children. A seedy-looking man of forty-five served as principal. He disclosed that about twenty-five years ago he had finished high school but had not gone beyond. During the war he worked as a tool-and-die cutter in one of the factories. When the war ended, he became weary of machine-shop work. He heard that teachers were needed, and so:

"I saw the county superintendent and he hired me. I've been here a couple months now. Never taught a day before in my life. It was hard at first, not knowing how to make out a schedule and such things, but I figured out what to do. I done the whole thing without any help."

The ex-mechanic hushed his noisy children—he had thirty-four of them in grades six, seven, and eight. The room was a mess. Apple cores and dirty milk bottles were strewn over the floor. A potbellied stove gave off acrid smoke that brought tears to one's eyes.

"Quiet down there, keep quiet," he barked.

Then he continued: "I wasn't showed one thing how to conduct a school. But it just came natural to me as if I had taught all my life."

"Any discipline problems?" I asked.

"None at all," he boasted. "I use a stick. See it in the corner? Cut 'em up now and then. I try to appeal to their intellect. If I can't, I wham 'em. They don't fight back. I see to that."

The principal, who is on an emergency substandard license, continued:

"Sure, sometimes I have to be rough. I handled one guy, he's fourteen, kind of tough yesterday. I had to wrastle with him and bang him up a bit. He's not at school today."

During this time the pupils were restive and began throwing chalk at each other. Barking at his students again, the principal remarked: "This is a tough section. Some of the kids get into trouble. I sent a fifteen-year-old girl home last week. She's going to have a baby."

Whether there is any connection between the juvenile delinquency in this principal's school and his harsh teaching methods a psychologist might be able to determine.

"I'm going to continue to teach, see," the ex-mechanic confided after he had quieted his class. "I don't want to go back to the shop. A poor element works there. A shop is the worst place that breeds discontent. See, I was out of my element. I don't want to associate with the low type.

"Let me explain, see. Church people have a different outlook on life than the come-and-go man. In the teaching profession, see, you meet the best classes of people. In the shop you meet the low type. They go to beer gardens and get the worst kind of social diseases. I don't care to work with a bunch of people like that. Eight out of ten of them have social diseases.

"I think the middle class of people is the type to teach school. They are the best type. The professional people, they are a good class of people to be with. It is the element I always wanted to work in."

Now the former tool-and-die operator is in his "element" and getting $35 a week for it. He is happy—but his young students looked sad and resentful.

Another teacher, this time in a Rocky Mountain state, looked like a female ancient mariner. She taught in a one-room rural school of thirty-four pupils. The ancient one gazed upon the visitor with bleared and watery eyes. The children threw spitballs and seemed to enjoy themselves. A more barren, desolate, sorry-looking classroom is difficult to imagine.

"What would you like to see?" asked the old woman. She explained that she had never taught before; had, in fact, never gone beyond the fifth grade herself, and that fifty-odd years ago. But the district needed a teacher—and she could use the $90 a month that comes nine months of the year.

"How about a civics lesson?" she suggested.

That seemed satisfactory enough.

Then began a discussion of good and bad laws, and how this country is ruled by stubborn men. Many things could—and in time, she had no doubt, would—be changed for the better.

"Wait till the women get the right to vote," she exclaimed in a seeming burst of inspiration. "Someday they will, and then our laws will be better than they are now."

Several of the older boys suppressed a chuckle, while one winked knowingly and tapped his forehead in a suggestive manner. But the mariner continued her civics lesson, not the least disturbed at the titters that swept through the shabby classroom.

In another school a young college graduate—he had attended an engineering school but failed as an engineer—was placed in charge of a one-room rural school. He was utterly lost. When the state supervisor arrived he found the engineer, a four days' growth of beard on his face, staring at the children who were romping around the yard.

"I'm glad you came," the engineer-teacher exclaimed. "I don't know how to open this school. I've been here three weeks and haven't had any class yet. How do you make out a daily schedule? What do you do first?"

After he was shown a few of the fundamentals of teaching, the children were called into the room. Ranging in age from six to fifteen years, they accepted their lot without protest. The supervisor spent several hours with the children, paying particular attention to the four first-graders, who had never been to school before that term.

As the supervisor left, the young engineer exclaimed:

"Gee, teaching must be fun if you know how!"

In another school, this time in central Georgia, one of the parents protested the appointment of a new teacher. The mother insisted that she would take her child out of the seventh grade in the small rural school where she was attending.

"Why, what's the trouble?" she was asked.

"I know the new teacher," she replied bitterly. "She was reared in this county. And I know that she has not gone beyond the fourth grade. What is the sense of letting my seventh-grade child be taught by a teacher who has not gone that far herself?"

Frankly, I had no answer.

Admitting that the question of incompetent teachers plagues the entire state, Dr. M. D. Collins, Georgia superintendent of schools, observed:

"Some of the emergency teachers just serve as caretakers."

A county superintendent in the same state said:

"We have a preacher who teaches school. I think he's had a year of high school education. Maybe less."

"Don't you know the educational qualifications of your teachers?" I asked in surprise.

"No, we don't ask candidates any more how much schooling they have had," he replied. "We're thankful to get teachers of any kind. They might resent it if we pried too much into their education."

A talk with the teacher-preacher disclosed that he had completed the second year in high school. He now taught twenty-eight children in the seventh grade. Stiff and ill at ease, he went through the motions of teaching.

"They are just bubbling over with energy," he said, waving his arms awkwardly in the direction of the students. "I have to hold them down. I preach every Saturday and Sunday. In school I give the children *lessings* in English, history, geography, arithmetic, and spelling."

For his work he receives $67.50 a month, nine months of the year.

Not all the emergency teachers are incompetent. Many of them are qualified, but lack one or two technical requirements or have insufficient experience for a regular license. In some states teachers, even though they are badly needed, are not employed unless they are college graduates.

On the whole, though, the 125,000 emergency teachers are poorer than the regular teachers. They do not measure up to the standards expected of teachers in an atomic age. They are not much better than the teachers of a century ago, when the schoolmaster, ridiculed and scorned, barely eked out an existence. Professional standards are going rapidly downhill. Every state has its long list of substandard teachers. School authorities are hopeful that they will soon be replaced with regular instructors.

But as has been seen, it is extremely doubtful whether an adequate supply of teachers will be available during the next five years. It is altogether likely that the emergency teachers will be frozen into their jobs, thus perpetuating the present incompetent teaching standards for years to come. On a smaller scale a similar situation existed after the last war, when several thousand teachers of low ability were given emergency licenses. Many of them are still in the system. Educators have estimated that they are responsible for the inadequate teaching given to many thousands of American youth during the last quarter century.

Numerous warnings have been issued against the employment of submarginal teachers. Dr. A. C. Flora, past president of the National Education Association and superintendent of schools, Columbia, South Carolina, declares: "Incompetent teachers now entering the school systems will permanently lower the nation's educational standards."

Certification officers will have the tremendous task, in the years ahead, of eliminating the emergency licenses. In some instances the emergency teacher, through in-service work or upgrading courses, will be able to reach the state's minimum requirements. In others, the teacher will be so incompetent and so deficient in the necessary educational background that his license will have to be revoked. At all costs the children must be protected against poorly qualified teachers.

We cannot continue to submit the nation's pupils to an inferior brand of teaching. The two million youngsters who are now receiving an inadequate schooling, and the five million who are not getting as good an education as they might, deserve our attention. Only by ridding the public school system of substandard teachers will we eliminate substandard training for our children.

Educators freely admit that this will not be an easy task. Not until more students go into the teaching profession will it be possible to replace the incompetent men and women with qualified teachers. In the meantime, though, it is well to remember that many of the emergency teachers are in the system at the behest of the community. Many are teaching as a public service and will be happy enough to step aside when their replacements are available. At the same time, the community must become aware of what is happening within its own schoolhouse. The community must make an inventory of its teachers, to discover which ones are doing an adequate job, which ones should be weeded out in the interests of the children.

One of the major tasks facing American education today is that of raising teaching standards. When every teacher in the country has a college degree and has undergone a strenuous training for his post, then teaching will receive the same acclaim and respect that medicine, engineering, and law command today.

Since 1941 more than 350,000 teachers have left the classroom. For the most part, they were the experienced, hardworking, ambitious teachers who were doing the best classroom job. This unprecedented exodus from the nation's schools has alarmed school officials everywhere. Nor has the exodus stopped. This year, it is predicted, another 75,000 teachers will leave. And next year, too.

To understand the serious nature of the crisis, it is necessary to realize that the 350,000 teachers who left were over and above those who would ordinarily leave for various causes. Normally there is a 10 per cent turnover in the teaching profession. Of the nation's 850,000 teachers, about 90,000 leave each year. Today 20 per cent of the teachers are leaving their classes, or one out of every five.

Everywhere I found the problem of high turnover uppermost in the minds of the school leaders. Superintendents and school officials agreed that, unless checked, it would lead to an unstable and weakened school system. Many superintendents told me that they had four, five, six, or more teachers in a single class in one term. The children sometimes found a new teacher before them every other week.

Typical of what is happening, and quite in keeping with present-day conditions, is the story told by a former teacher, now on the staff of the University of Denver. Recently she had been a teacher at a junior high school in a Tennessee school.

"I taught art, although I had never taught that subject before in my life," she explained. "I received $3 a day for the work—and had to climb four flights of stairs to class. The principal told me I was the sixth art teacher that he had employed that term. I stayed five weeks—and left."

Why did she leave?

"Teachers are afraid of what staying in the system long will do to them," she said. "They wonder if they are really being fair to themselves by remaining in school. You can't get excited in your teaching job any more. People talk about the schools being the arsenals of democracy, but that is a lot of talk. More persons will go into teaching when they feel that it is a real profession and that they will be treated with respect."

Similar observations came from teachers in various parts of the country. They work for a while at low salaries, amid insufferable conditions, subjected to community scrutiny—and then they leave to go into another profession, or take another job. Never before have so many persons left any profession. And never before has the rate of turnover of those who remain on the job been so great.

The pity of it is that for the most part the best teachers have left or are leaving. The top-notch teachers, those who have made a name for themselves, are offered more money by industry or the government—and they quit. It is true that their places are filled, but all too frequently their substitutes are inferior and poorly qualified.

Even before the war the turnover rate was high enough to cause concern. When one out of every ten teachers in service has to be replaced each year, something is basically wrong. This is not an enviable record nor one that can fill us with pride. By way of contrast Great Britain finds it necessary to replace one out of every thirty-three teachers; of the 200,000 teachers in that country, only 6,000 leave or are retired annually. That makes for stability and higher professional standards. A 3 per cent turnover, as compared with our normal 10 per cent and now our war and postwar 20 per cent, is an indictment of our school system that cannot be lightly brushed aside. Where the turnover is within reason, it is possible to select teachers with greater care and to prepare them more effectively for continued and competent service. The present turnover in the American teaching staff is entirely too high for the good of the school system.

Even before the war, teaching in this country had not gained the status of a profession. Too often both men and women selected teaching not as a lifetime profession, but as a stopgap until something better came along—or in the case of the women teachers, until they found a husband. One school commissioner said ruefully, as he finished appointing his eighth substitute teacher that term for the third grade:

"Before the war I used to think that the teachers who came to me were just a mob of mobile maidens meditating matrimony. Now the profession has become a procession of men and women passing through my school system, stopping just long enough to catch their breath and pass on to the next larger town where they can get more money."

Exaggerated, of course, but there is enough truth in that statement to make American citizens think. Too many persons consider the teaching profession in terms of a one- or two-year stopgap on their way toward success elsewhere.

Public school teaching in this country has always been a woman's profession. The overwhelming majority of teachers, particularly on the elementary level, are women. However, in the decade prior to Pearl Harbor, more men had begun to enter teaching. This was especially true on the high school level and to some extent in the elementary and junior high school grades. Then, during the war, the number of men teaching in our public schools dropped considerably. Nearly 100,000 went into the Army. Few men were enrolled in the teachers' colleges.

With the return of peacetime conditions, the men have boycotted the schools. Both on the elementary and secondary levels fewer men are now in the classroom than ever before. Many of the veterans have not returned to their former school posts.

Why do teachers leave the profession?

A woman elementary schoolteacher in a small West Virginia town gave this answer, indicative of the unrest found elsewhere:

"West Virginia schools are facing a crisis. Our best teachers are leaving for better-paying jobs or have gone to near-by states where the pay is better. Several thousand West Virginia boys and girls of school age are not enrolled in any school because of the critical teacher shortage. Many thousands are taught by people with less than high school training, and substandard teachers are the rule rather than the exception.

"Our buildings and equipment are old and worn out. Rural schools particularly are in very bad condition. We need a merit system whereby inefficient teachers can be weeded out. We also need higher standards for teachers to prevent those with emergency or very low certificates from undermining what there is left of the profession. Above all, we need more and better supervision."

Another teacher, twenty-five years in the profession, explained why she is ready to leave. She is now a kindergarten teacher in a mid-western state.

"I have forty-four children in the morning and forty-five in the afternoon," she said. "By the end of the morning I am whipped. I just can't go on. We don't have the equipment we need; we have no modern supplies. I can only be a policeman and keep the children from yelling too much. I've been teaching kindergarten classes for twenty-five years and there's been no improvement in all that time."

This teacher takes home $139.67 a month, ten months a year. The other two months she works as a clerk at a hotel; one summer she was a waitress. She's not sure that she'll continue teaching—maybe she'll take the offer of the local settlement house and leave teaching entirely.

Teachers who quit the profession explain that they don't want to become "stuck" in a job that all too often leads them into a blind alley. The general conception of a typical teacher is not very complimentary, others complain. There has been too much caricaturing of teachers in the press, on the radio, and through the movies, others say. Plainly, teachers need a sound public-relations program to restore their prestige.

"We are considered to be queer old maids or tough battle-axes," one of the teachers complained. "There is little prestige today in being a teacher. We are pitied rather than honored."

Whatever the reason, nearly 40 per cent of the teachers have rushed from the school systems of the nation in five years. At the same time, 20 per cent of the teachers each year are leaving their present jobs for new ones, either in education or outside the profession. Unless this trend is stopped, all of the best teachers will soon be out of the schools. Educators recognize that this would leave the nation's schools in an exceedingly dangerous position. They are concerned at the stampede from the classrooms.

Unless the teachers' confidence is restored, American public schools will continue to deteriorate. The present crisis will grow worse. Our schools were not bombed as were the European schools. But more than two years after the end of the war they are being wrecked just as surely as though they had been blasted by a fleet of heavy bombers.

Various state and local officials are concerned with this difficult problem. They are eager to make teaching more attractive so that the rate of turnover will come down. They know that as long as teachers stay in the profession for a year or two, and then leave for other jobs, the profession will be unable to show any improvement. In some instances the turnover has been almost complete—Missouri, for example, reported that only 2 per cent of its present teachers were in the system in 1940-41. This means an almost 100 per cent turnover in six years. In other states, such as North Carolina, only 33 per cent, or about one-third, of all the teachers who were teaching in the state in 1941 were still there six years later.

Because so many are leaving, the number of new teachers employed by the schools each year has steadily increased. During 1946-47, for example, Kentucky hired 50 per cent new teachers for the schools of the state. In Nevada 45 per cent of the teachers during that year were new to the state. Idaho had a turnover of 40 per cent. It is difficult to see how the school systems in those states can be strengthened or improved as long as the teachers leave the profession in such large numbers.

A five-point program to improve education, and at the same time keep the teachers from deserting the classroom, is outlined by Dr. M. D. Collins, Georgia state superintendent of schools:

1. Adequate appropriations to effectuate the present expanded state program including the 50 per cent increase in teachers' salaries.
2. Establishment of a plan for awarding liberal scholarships or free tuition to one or more students from each county who are qualified by ability and aptitude for teaching.
3. Enactment of permissive legislation providing for a twelfth grade in Georgia's public school system.
4. Establishment of a school-building equalization fund to aid the poorer rural counties in erecting needed school facilities.
5. Matching of federal funds in full for vocational education, which includes vocational agriculture, vocational home economics, trades and industries, distributive education, and occupational information and guidance.

Although this is a state program, and applicable in large measure only to Georgia, nonetheless it does offer a guide to other states. Here, as elsewhere, the problem is to stabilize the teaching profession, by making it attractive to young men and women.

Typical of what is happening throughout the nation is the experience found in Maryland. Within a ten-year period the percentage of teachers new to Maryland county schools more than doubled. The figures from 1936 to 1946, taken year by year, indicate a trend that has caused deep concern to all who are interested in the welfare of the nation's schools.

| | | Maryland teachers new to: | | |
| | County high schools | | County elementary schools | |
YEAR	NO.	PERCENTAGE	NO.	PERCENTAGE
1936	199	13.3	204	7.4
1937	241	15.0	207	7.5
1938	233	13.8	202	7.4
1939	255	14.4	203	.7.4
1940	269	15.0	215	8.0
1941	402	21.6	266	10.1
1942	456	24.5	362	13.6
1943	587	31.9	565	21.2
1944	521	29.1	521	19.3
1945	525	29.0	553	19.8
1946	779	37.0	621	22.8

The above pattern can be duplicated anywhere in the country. Within a ten-year period nearly one-third of the high school and elementary teachers left their jobs and had to be replaced by teachers from other sources, many of them inferior to those whose jobs they took. In a number of Maryland counties the per cent of teachers new to their jobs ran well above 50, while in one county 124 per cent of the teachers were new! A complete turnover of the teaching staff within one year is not conducive to good school administration nor effective educational procedure.

Comments from leaders in the field show conclusively that the turnover is harming the morale of the system and at the same time forcing school superintendents to appoint men and women to their staffs who in previous years would not be acceptable. Typical is the observation made by Superintendent Arthur Gould of the Boston, Massachusetts, school system. Many of his top-notch teachers, some with master's or doctor's degrees, have left to get better-paying positions elsewhere. The new appointments frequently do not measure up to the quality of those being replaced.

"The fundamental task that confronts any community is the

education of its children," Dr. Gould observes. "We can't give our children a decent education if we do not get the best possible teachers. That is a major problem that deserves our utmost attention."

In answer to the question: "What do you consider to be your best source today of well-qualified new teachers?", 450 of the leading school superintendents replied:

Other school systems .... 43 per cent
State teachers' colleges .... 37 per cent
Liberal arts colleges .... 8 per cent
Commercial placement agencies .... 11 per cent

More than 40 per cent of the teachers whom city superintendents appoint each year come from other school systems. The implications of that fact are both grave and revealing. If this "stealing" continues, a tremendous void will result in the school systems that cannot compete with the big cities. Obviously, an insufficient number of teachers are being trained at present to meet the demands of the schools. It will take many years before we can approach the stability found in Great Britain, or in any one of the other major countries of the world. To be a schoolmaster in France, Belgium, or Italy is a mark of distinction. Teachers know that they have a lifetime job. A similar attitude is necessary in this country.

Plainly, teachers in this country must have a professional status comparable to the other professions. If the rate of turnover continues, the profession of teaching will lose the respect of both the teachers and the public.

FREQUENTLY cited as the number one problem in the public school system, the question of money disturbs more teachers than any other single issue. The average American classroom teacher, in the year 1947, received $2,000 a year, or just about $40 a week. Rural teachers earned less than $30 weekly. Low as these salaries are, they represent substantial increases over prewar figures. Before Pearl Harbor the average teacher received about $1,400 a year; the rural schoolteacher was content with less than $1,000.

Despite a gradual increase in the last five years, the teachers of this country are the financial stepchildren of the public. Averages, however, mean very little to the individual teacher. Despite inflationary prices, 10,000 teachers today still get less than $12 a week! Another 200,000 get $25 weekly or less. More than half the teachers of the country get below $40.

Teachers are up in arms over the salaries they receive. For the first time in educational history the schoolteachers have become noisy. They are demanding that their salaries be increased. Many communities have raised the salaries of teachers. In some instances the increases have been substantial; in others merely a token payment to quiet the teaching staff.

Educators as well as laymen agree that the teachers do not get enough money to compensate them for their long professional training and the work that they do. Somehow a peculiar set of values has arisen in this country. Teachers get less money for cultivating the minds of children than garbage collectors do for picking up waste or street cleaners for keeping the streets tidy.

In one of the southern states a teacher sent this letter to his superintendent:

"Dear Sir: I don't think I'll teach any more. I'm now earning $8.25 weekly. I can't get married on that. I reckon I'll go to work on the Atlantic Coast Line Railroad. They pay section hands $7 a day.

"If you can pay more, write me. I like to teach. If not, I'll be over Tuesday with the books and blackboard."

This young teacher was offered a 50 per cent increase in his salary. He remained on his job, and at last account has not turned in his books or his blackboard. I'm not certain, though, that his increased salary permitted him to get married.

Although teachers have received increases, they point to the still greater increases received by those in industry. They complain of the high cost of living. They insist that on the basis of actual dollars, they are receiving less than before the war.

Comparisons with other professions may be fallacious, but the teachers point to the salaries received by those with less training as evidence that they are not pampered by the community. During the war it was not uncommon for high school boys and girls, working part time, to make more than their teachers working full time. Today the average teacher gets less than is paid to a good secretary.

In one state, when the question of salaries came up, the chairman of the education department asked: "What do our teachers get a year?"

"About $20 a week," he was informed.

"Impossible! My office boy gets more than that," he exclaimed. And then he agreed to an increase in salaries for the teachers.

But that is not the typical reaction. In another state, informed that the teachers were demanding a substantial increase in salaries, the legislative leader snapped:

"If teachers don't like the pay they are getting, they have their God-given right to quit."

Evidently he didn't know the facts in his own state—for that is exactly what they were doing. Seventy-five per cent had quit in four years. They left to go into all sorts of jobs that paid them more money although frequently gave them less satisfaction.

Perhaps Detroit can be taken as a typical example of how the community neglects its teachers. Some light on this question can be shed through a comparison of the salaries of prison cooks at the city's jail, comfort station attendants, dogcatchers, animal keepers at the zoo, garbage collectors, and rat exterminators, with that of a beginning-teacher salary in the public schools.

The prison cook gets a beginning salary of $2,736 in Detroit; comfort station attendants in any of the city's numerous comfort stations get $2,222. The dogcatcher gets $2,485 and in a short time is able to receive a salary of $3,120. The zoo's animal keepers get $2,496 at the start for their ability to feed the tigers and keep away from their paws. The garbage collector foremen get $4,761 and by showing improvement and regular attendance, interest in their job, and similar traits, can eventually reach $5,238. The rat exterminator foreman begins at $3,095 and whether or not he kills his quota of rats he can easily reach a maximum of $3,492.

Detroit's schoolteachers, in common with teachers everywhere, do not fare so well as many of these people. They begin at a salary of $2,094 only after they have completed a minimum of four years of college and have shown unusual ability in guiding children, plus a superior knowledge of one or more specific subjects. In terms of the take-home pay, Detroit teachers receive slightly in excess of $8.25 a day on a twenty-day-per-month basis. This is less than that same teacher would have to pay for menial housework were she to hire someone to clean the house. This, of course, would not include home cooking and laundry. After seven years Detroit teachers can reach their maximum of $3,520 or, if they have gone to college an extra year and earned a master's degree, they can realize a maximum of $3,620 in eight years.

Still, of course, not on a par with the garbage collector foreman!

Or take New Orleans. The dogcatcher gets from $1,500 to $1,820 a year, depending on his speed. The salary of the prison cooks is $1,500—and it may soon be raised to $2,160. The zoo keeper's standard salary is $2,400 a year.

The teacher starts at $1,400.

"Frequently our head professors call in carpenters or plumbers to do odd jobs in the classroom," a college president told me. "Much to their chagrin, they find that the mechanics, the carpenters, or the plumbers get considerably more money than they do."

As a case in point, he related how the chairman of the physics department wanted to install a new light in the laboratory. He called in a technician who was a member of a local union. The physics professor, who had earned a distinguished name for himself in his field, learned that the electrician was making $8,500 a year. The professor thought himself fortunate at his $6,500 figure! It had taken world recognition to bring him that sum.

Teachers receive less money for their work than do most of the other professional groups. The average in 1941 for lawyers employed on a salary basis was $4,683; the average salaried physician received $5,495. In 1941 the average teacher received $1,470. The disparity between these groups has grown considerably since then. Even though the teacher averages close to $2,000, the other professions have gone proportionately higher.

Nation-wide, the teacher does not fare so well financially as almost any other worker in the community. This fact was disclosed in a questionnaire, sent by *The New York Times,* to 450 representative city- and rural-school superintendents. Fifty per cent of the superintendents indicated that teachers receive either lower or about the same salaries as unskilled laborers.

In 53 per cent of the cities the teachers get less money than truck drivers; in 74 per cent they receive less than carpenters. The superintendents reported that in 94 per cent of the communities the teachers' average salaries were less than lawyers'; in 94 per cent, less than doctors', and in 92 per cent, less than engineers'.

During 1946 the average salary for government workers was $2,595. Professional employees of the government received $4,150, with a starting salary of $2,695. The teachers, during the same period, received an annual average salary of $1,900.

A survey among a cross section of New York City teachers, where the pay is among the highest in the country, shows that 80 per cent of the teachers have been unable to save during the past two years; many have had their savings wiped out. One-fifth have gone into debt.

In New York the present starting salaries for teachers, under the new schedule adopted by the 1947 state legislature, is just about $50 a week, or $2,500 annually. New York City employers recently granted these wages to other occupational groups:

Truck drivers .... $62.90 a week
Clothing workers 61.00
Printers 66.50
Newspaper reporters 90.00
Bartenders 50.00

Elevator operators in office buildings. .$1,660 to $2,019 a year

Building construction workers recently agreed to a general over-all salary of $100 a week.

The long vacations and holiday sessions no longer compensate for poor salaries. Many teachers work during the summer or hold afternoon jobs in order to supplement their school salaries. In one New Jersey community thirty-eight of fifty-six teachers worked in the afternoon or during the summer. Their jobs ranged from hotel chambermaids to bartenders. A survey of 2,800 New York City schoolteachers showed that 90 per cent

of the male teachers and 20 per cent of the women took outside jobs in 1945-46. A sampling of thirty men teachers in a
California city showed that twenty are working outside of their
regular jobs. One has a full-time night job. One runs a linotype
machine. Another is a basketball coach. Teachers in that city
get $60 a week.

"How can we live on that and support a family?" a veteran
who recently returned to the system asked. "I have a wife and
three children. When I came back to this city I found the
rentals were beyond reason. In desperation I took a furnished
apartment for which I pay $100 a month. It's pretty tough
trying to stretch a $60 salary to cover your expenses. After the
taxes, pension, and other deductions are made, I get less than
$50 a week to take home. Do you blame me for selling shoes
on the side?"

A typical complaint comes from the classroom teachers of a
North Carolina town. The daily take-home pay of a Class-A
teacher—one who has a college degree and has had courses in
practice teaching—is $3.15 after one year's experience; $3.85
after five years; and $4.41 after ten years.

A study made by the New York State Teachers Association,
an organization with 44,000 members, disclosed that the majority of teachers in the organization were in debt. One man
had to sell his cemetery lots to pay his bills; another teacher,
a man of fifty with two children to support, took a job in a
hotel where he is now scrubbing floors. These are not unusual
cases. Their plight could be multiplied a hundredfold in all
parts of the country.

Among the supplementary jobs held by the New York teachers—and their experience can be duplicated almost everywhere—are these: truck driver, welder, clerical millworker, bill
collector, shoe salesman, organist, waitress, dance band leader,
summer theater manager, florist, choir director, ticket seller,
sign hanger, real estate salesman, carpenter, telephone operator, photographer, milkman, headwaiter, gardener, cook, nurse-
maid, moving picture operator, window decorator, barber,

handy man, chambermaid, mailman, hospital worker, station helper, tax clerk, cashier, landscaper, policeman, lifeguard, hostess, dressmaker, taxi driver, bartender, town assessor, ditch-digger, and bus driver.

The teacher had to utilize his time, which should have gone into professional improvement, to earn money so that he could support his family, or keep out of debt. It is difficult to know, in many instances, whether a man is a teacher or a ditchdigger, when he makes more each week digging ditches than he does teaching children! The teachers are ready to undertake any type of work if it will help them earn a living. Plainly, teaching alone cannot do that under existing salary conditions.

Sixty former teachers in Chicago are now working as waitresses or dice-game girls—and for their work earn from $36 to $70 a week plus meals. In West Virginia, a teacher with a salary of $178 a month was suspended for digging coal on the side. He made $320 a month for his part-time job. A band-master and a music teacher in Providence, Rhode Island, worked at a gas station after school hours. A Tennessee school principal worked Saturdays as a grocery clerk; a teacher hired out as a cotton picker, while still another took on baby sitting as a side line. Many teachers work in department stores or type manuscripts for additional money. In Brooklyn a veteran, who returned to his teaching job at $50 a week, found that he needed more money to support his family. He took on an evening job as bartender, for which he received $60 a week. A social science teacher, father of two children, took a job as a commercial photographer. An industrial arts teacher, the father of five children, supplemented his income by making period furniture, while another art teacher took up free-lance lettering and commercial sign writing.

Not all teachers are able to work in their spare time—they have a household to run and children of their own to raise. Typical is the case of a teacher in Utica, New York, who observes:

"I have been unable to work summers due to the fact that

I have four children—two are young—who had to be cared for. Consequently for the last three summers since my husband's death, I have gone into debt so badly that it takes the best part of the next year's salary to get straightened out again.

"It is a ghastly and vicious circle, and if help isn't forthcoming soon, some of us will be completely submerged. Not much publicity has been given the widowed teacher. Trying to support four children and myself on the salary of a grade teacher is something that won't bear thinking about. It just can't be done. And always before me looms the question: 'How am I to educate them?'"

A Buffalo teacher, father of two children, in the high school system for twenty-four years, is now selling vacuum cleaners in the afternoon and evening. It keeps him out of the house and away from his family from seven in the morning until midnight—but he needs the money.

"I've made more selling vacuum cleaners in the last two months than I did teaching," he confessed. "I take home $50 a week from school. How can I support my wife and young boys on that?"

"I'd love to go to summer school and finish up work for my master's degree," another teacher said to me wistfully. "I only need eight points and I could do that in a six-week term. But I can't afford to go. Even my part-time work at Sears, Roebuck isn't enough to see me through."

In one of the larger cities of the country a high school science teacher, twenty-eight years in service, turned to me and said indignantly: "Look at my bank balance! After all these years I've been able to save $51.45. Every two weeks the school takes out $1.50 for war savings bonds. In any other profession I'd be getting ready to retire. But what have I ahead of me as a teacher?"

I talked to a high school instructor who had been teaching for thirty-five years. I spent several hours in his home—met his wife and three children.

"After thirty-five years I am making $45 a week," he said

bitterly. "I've studied to be a teacher. I have two degrees from the best universities in the country. They tell me I have succeeded in my job. I am head of the chemistry department. Men come to me for advice from the industrial firms for miles around. In any other profession I'd be a failure if after thirty-five years I was making the pay I now get."

"My goodness, it's difficult to get along on what my husband makes," his wife broke in. "We're always broke. I haven't had a new dress in six years. I have to watch every penny."

This is not an isolated case. I spoke to countless teachers who had similar stories to tell.

Calling upon the public for support, the teachers point out that the money they get for teaching is insufficient to live on; many depend upon their families or friends for partial support. During the summer the teachers work at odd jobs. Selling encyclopedias and magazine subscriptions are common methods. Teachers frequently boast that they can make as much in ten summer weeks as they do in ten school months of full-time teaching. The old quip "I'm working my way through school," takes on added significance when it is uttered by a patient schoolteacher eking out a living by selling magazine subscriptions.

Educators have voiced their opposition to these conditions so long that it no longer attracts attention. Typical is the statement of Dr. David H. Patton, superintendent of schools at Syracuse, New York, who observes:

"When we pay charwomen more than we pay teachers, we are not going to buy the best brain power to teach our children."

Similarly, Dr. Harold F. Clark of Teachers College, Columbia University, one of the nation's foremost educational economists, warns that unless salaries are doubled the present acute teacher shortage will continue and disastrous social and educational conditions will result in a few years.

"Unskilled labor last year was paid more than teachers," Dr. Clark points out. "Today there is a shortage of 100,000 teach-

ers. Not enough are entering the profession to replace those
who leave, while many who are trained as teachers avoid practice because of the salary situation. Neither the nation nor the
teaching profession can afford to permit these conditions to
continue.

"The story of the teacher's situation must be gotten across
to the American public. The teacher must have his salary
doubled at the outset and then discussion may start over the
amount of increase above that. Unless the teacher's salary is
adjusted we will go down farther and farther on the scale of
ability in recruiting teachers."

Dr. Clark holds that such salaries as $2,000 and $3,000 no
longer make sense in today's economic picture. Salaries of
$5,000, $6,000, and $7,000 must be normal and routine in the
classroom, he is convinced.

"The public is not aware of the calamity that has hit the
schools," Dr. Clark warns. "Otherwise the schools would not be
allowed to deteriorate. If the schools had been destroyed 150
years ago our economy could have continued. That is not true
today in our complex technological civilization. Without education our kind of world cannot exist. The present teachers'
salaries are in the bottom half of salaries paid to all workers in
the country. If you keep this up long enough you will draw
your teachers from the bottom half of our population. If we
want to get as able teachers as we had in 1939, we will have
to double their salaries. And remember, we were not getting
the best quality then."

Although the average salary on a nation-wide basis is slightly
less than $40 a week, twelve states pay an average of less than
$30. Another twelve pay less than $35 weekly. The teachers find
it impossible to live normal, wholesome lives on the money
they earn. They are constantly worrying and fretting about
bills that must be paid and insurance premiums that must be
met. It does not take a psychologist to recognize that this constant worry and fear of debt hurts them as teachers. A calm,

contented teacher will make a better, more understanding individual in the classroom.

"I take home $74 every two weeks, ten months a year," a Massachusetts teacher said. "Since I have to pay for a room and eat all my meals out, I have to budget the $37 a week very carefully. As principal of my school I have an added responsibility. I feel as though I'm never through. Every night I have papers to correct and my lessons to prepare for the next day.

"How I envy my friends who finish their work at five o'clock! A teacher's job is never done. Maybe if I got more money—say, if my check were $150 instead of $74—I might stick it out. As it is, I'm planning to quit this spring."

In addition to demands for increased salaries, the teachers in many cities are campaigning to introduce the "single-salary schedule." At present in many school systems the high school teachers receive the highest salaries, the junior high school teachers receive less, and the elementary teachers receive the least, regardless of preparation. That is, an elementary teacher with a doctor of philosophy degree will get less than a high school teacher in the same system who has only a bachelor's degree.

The greatest impetus for the single-salary principle has come recently from New York State. A single schedule, to cover all teachers regardless of grades taught, based entirely on amount of preparation and merit of teaching, has been established. The range goes from $2,000 to $5,400. Automatic increases go to all teachers until the sixth year; at that time 50 per cent of the teachers will be permitted to go to the next higher bracket. Elementary teachers have been pleading for the single-salary schedule for many years.

Within recent years three of the large cities adopted the single schedule—Cleveland, St. Louis, and Newark, N. J. Prior to 1946, the single-salary schedule was in effect in Detroit, Milwaukee, New Orleans, Minneapolis, Cincinnati, Indianapolis, and Kansas City, Missouri. Professional and school groups for the most part support the teachers' plea for equal pay. They point out that the elementary teachers have the children the first eight years of their school life; during this time they can do a tremendous amount of good—or harm. The National Emergency Conference on Teacher Preparation and Supply, meeting in Chautauqua in June, 1946, urged that equal pay be given for work done in elementary and secondary schools.

Various school groups and professional organizations are urging that a minimum salary schedule of $2,400 annually for all teachers be established. This minimum would increase in annual increments until a maximum of $4,000 to $5,000 would be reached.

There are bright spots on the horizon. Communities in all parts of the country are granting wage increases. Thirty-two states report that they plan definite state action to raise teachers' salaries. Heading the list, probably setting the pattern for other states, is California. By a thumping three-to-one majority, it approved a constitutional amendment fixing a minimum salary of $2,400 for all teachers in the state, rural as well as urban.

A sales-tax amendment, which will provide in the neighborhood of $30,000,000 additional funds to the Michigan schools, was adopted in 1946. In this case the teachers and parents worked closely together and despite opposition carried the amendment by a two-to-one majority. Oklahoma, too, approved new laws which permit the local school districts to impose higher taxes for school purposes; it likewise increased the state contributions to education and provided free textbooks. Oregon and Utah voted school laws designed to help the school system.

Although the process is slow, it is a hopeful one. With a $2,400 minimum—$46 a week—and salaries going up to $100 a week, it should be possible to attract qualified persons to the teaching profession. But as long as twelve states pay their teachers less than $30 a week, and another twelve less than

$35, and as long as half the teachers of America get less than
$40 a week, the profession will be decidedly unattractive.

One town in North Carolina has started a crusade to increase
the salaries of its teachers. To acquaint the "thinking citizenship" with facts concerning individual teacher pay, the classroom teachers' association made these pointed statements in
answer to the question: Did you know—

1. That teachers are paid 180 days out of the year, but must eat
   and pay board for 365 days?
2. That teachers are "docked" for being sick at the rate of $4 a
   day—pay that goes out of their salary for a substitute—and that
   this $4 is more than the annual daily take-home wage of the
   regular teacher with less than ten years of experience?
3. That if no substitute is available—a situation usually handled by
   having a student in charge of the class or having a fellow
   teacher double up—the salary still does not go to the teacher?
4. That when conditions exist that are beyond the teachers' control—such as schools closed because of bad roads or epidemics—
   the teachers are "laid off" without pay and yet are required to
   stay in the community on call, paying room and board?
5. That teachers receive no overtime pay, and yet are expected to
   spend after-school hours grading papers, conducting extracurricular activities, and preparing for the next day's work?
6. That the daily take-home pay of a teacher with ten years' experience is $4.41, or $.55 an hour?
7. That teachers are the only group who do not receive one single
   holiday with pay—not even Christmas?
8. That teachers receive not one cent from around June 10 to
   October 1?
9. That teachers are financially unable to carry retirement insurance?
10. That teachers, on those meager wages, are expected to dress
    neatly, attractively, and tastefully as an example to the
    children?

Frequently it is said: "Why are teachers fretting about
higher salaries? They have security and a soft berth. When a
depression comes they can sit pretty."

But that is not the case. During the depression teachers' salaries were slashed by as much as 50 per cent. Chicago may be taken as a typical example of what happened elsewhere. It will also provide the clue as to why the teachers are clamoring for higher salaries.

From 1928 to 1931 there were no changes in salary. From then on this is the story:

1932—reduce teacher salary 10.5 per cent
1933—salaries reduced 15 per cent
1934—reduction amounted to 23.5 per cent
1935—continue 15 per cent deduction from teachers' basic salaries and operate on a nine-month basis—amounting to 23.5 per cent
1936—reduction same as 1935
1937—reduction same as 1936
1938—restore one-half of 15 per cent deduction and operate schools on nine-and-one-half-month basis—reduction amounted to 21.8 per cent
1939—continue 7.5 per cent deduction from teachers' basic salaries and operate schools on nine-and-three-quarter-month year—reduction amounted to 12.1 per cent
1940—continue 7.5 per cent deduction from teachers' basic salaries and operate schools on ten-month year—reduction amounted to 7.5 per cent
1941—continue 7.5 per cent reduction
1942—reduce deductions to 5.5 per cent
1943—restoration of teachers' salaries to 1931 basis
1944—elementary teachers increased $125 a year
1945—no change in 1945
1946—elementary teachers increased $225 a year; high school teachers, $150

Compared with the increased cost of living the raises received by the teachers are negligible. Actually, they represent a substantial loss in real earning power. That is why many of the Chicago teachers have threatened to go out on strike, and have demanded that their salaries be increased still further.

They point out that from 1928 to 1944 they received no increase of any kind; in fact, during this period they received cuts that went as high as 23.5 per cent. Similarly, teachers elsewhere were cut during the depression. In some instances these reductions were restored only after a long and painful controversy.

For 1946-47 the salaries paid teachers were far out of line when compared with salaries paid any other profession, and almost any other trade or job. Mississippi, with an average salary of $15.47 for its teachers, stood at the bottom of the list, while the District of Columbia, with a $60.25 salary schedule, stood at the head. North Carolina and North Dakota paid their teachers an average of $27 a week, while Vermont went to $27.50. South Carolina could boast of only a $24.90 weekly salary. On the upper ranges were found New York State, with $59.96, Connecticut with $46.58, and Maryland, Massachusetts, and Washington, all at $46.

America is now exerting its democratic influence throughout the world. We cannot afford to maintain a staff of underpaid, incompetent schoolteachers.

THE United States spends less of its national income for education than Great Britain or the Union of Soviet Socialist Republics. During 1946, despite the inflationary boom period, this country spent about $2,500,000,000 for public school education, or not more than 1.5 per cent of its estimated income of $160,000,000,000. For the same period, Great Britain, with its impoverished economy, is estimated to have spent about 3 per cent. The Soviet Union averages around 8 per cent of its total income for education.

Frankly conceding that education is an important part of its Five-Year Plan, the Russian government increased its 1946-47 educational budget over the preceding year by 52 per cent. Its 1947 budget calls for an appropriation of $7,500,000,000 for education, out of a total budget of $60,000,000,000. In addition, several billions more were allocated for health protection, physical culture, and allied educational projects.

The Soviet Union boasts that in the year 1946-47 a total of 23,339,000 pupils attended elementary and secondary schools, or 13.9 per cent more than the previous year. By the end of the 1947 semester there will be 653,000 students attending higher institutions of learning, and 1,030,000 in technical schools. The number in higher educational establishments has increased 22.6 per cent and in technical schools by 22.9 per cent over 1945.

It is of value for Americans to know that the primary emphasis is being placed by the Soviet Union on the training of specialists for new fields of science and engineering. Under the

Five-Year Plan, Russia proposes to graduate 120,000 engineers and 347,000 technicians for industry and construction; 47,000 persons in higher education and 198,000 in secondary education for agriculture; 98,000 doctors and 284,000 medical personnel with secondary education.

During the same five-year period the United States will prepare fewer than 100,000 engineers, a handful of agricultural specialists, and about 20,000 doctors. Plainly this country is being rapidly outdistanced by the Soviet Union in the amount of money spent for education and in the number of trained personnel being prepared. According to Sergei Kaftanov, Minister of Higher Education of the U.S.S.R., a student body of 550,000 attended 806 institutions of higher learning in the academic year 1945-46.

"While the Soviet Union today has more students in higher education institutions than all the countries of Europe combined, considerable expansion of our higher education program must be accomplished to meet the nation's needs," the Soviet Minister reports. "The 70,000 young specialists who were awarded degrees this year are only one-fifth of the number needed."

Many educators and laymen are concerned at the lack of financial support that education is receiving in this country. They say that if Russia can spend seven and one-half billion dollars for education to ensure the continuance of its communistic form of government, the United States can do no less to spread knowledge of democracy among the youth of the land.

Ironically enough, the United States spent a greater percentage of its national income for education during the depression than it does today. Although in actual dollars there has been a slight increase in money spent, in percentages the amount has sagged steadily until now it is probably at a new low.

Back in the first boom days of 1929 our national income reached $83,000,000,000. That year the United States spent

2.7 per cent of its income for public schools. Then came the depression; during 1932, with the national income down to $40,000,000,000, we spent two billion dollars for our schools, or 5 per cent of the total national income. At present, with the national income nearly four times our depression low, the United States is spending less than it did in the past.

In the postwar period, with science, engineering, and technical developments playing a considerable part in the war and peace program of the nation, it is tragic, if not suicidal, for this country to permit its schools to starve. Nourishment, in the form of dollars, is necessary to keep the public schools alive.

Authorities in the field recommend that a 5 per cent investment of our national income for education is essential in the atomic age. On that basis the country would spend seven and one-half billion dollars for schools, assuming that we reach a stabilized 150 billion dollar income. At that, our expenditures would not exceed the money being spent for schools by the Soviet Union.

At present the money spent for the support of education in this country is far less than that spent for liquor, tobacco, or cosmetics. In 1945 the United States spent $7,700,000,000 for alcoholic beverages, or $55.65 per capita of population. At the same time we spent about $2,500,000,000 for elementary and secondary schools, or $17.76 per capita. Tobacco, too, came out ahead of the support for public schools. In 1945 we spent three billion dollars for tobacco, or $21.49 per capita of population. The figure is much higher today. Beauty and barbershop services, together with toilet preparations, came to just about the figure we spend for schools.

Can the United States afford to spend more money for education? Both the Chamber of Commerce and the National Association of Manufacturers have urged that the schools receive greater support. An extensive study conducted by the education committee of the Chamber of Commerce, entitled *Education—an Investment in People,* shows conclusively that there is a substantial and positive correlation between the amount a state spends for its public schools and the social and economic level it reaches.

In its study the Chamber of Commerce shows that there is a relationship between the money a state spends for education and the amount of retail sales, the circulation of magazines, and the number of telephones in the state. Thirty-one states hold identical group positions in both level of education and per capita retail sales, while thirty-two states hold identical group positions in both educational level and circulation of magazines.

An indication of the relationship between money spent for education and the economic prosperity of a community, as brought out by the Chamber of Commerce, can be seen in these illustrations:

The average annual school expenditure per pupil in Nevada in 1910, 1920, and 1930 was $102; in Mississippi it was $21. The average retail sales per capita for those years were $564 in Nevada, $129 in Mississippi.

Magazine circulation for each thousand population was 509 in Nevada and 104 in Mississippi. Moreover, Nevada had 175 telephones per thousand population to thirty-six for Mississippi.

Comparable relations exist between educational expenditures and the indices of economic prosperity. From the point of view of dollars and cents, education pays for itself. This country, the Chamber of Commerce has shown, can afford to educate its children. On the basis of its study, the Chamber reaches these significant conclusions:

"Education is an essential instrument through which commerce, industry, and agriculture can be expanded in rising degree.

"The cost of adequate education is an investment that local citizens and business can well afford in increased measure, when related step by step to the improvement of local economic conditions."

Similarly, the National Association of Manufacturers at its

last congress passed a resolution calling upon the communities to support education to a greater degree than is now the case, and urged that more money be given to the teachers. The National Association of Manufacturers, like the Chamber of Commerce, considers support of public education to be a sound investment.

Educators and businessmen are convinced that the United States can afford to spend more money for education. During the war years expenditures for both luxuries and necessities increased phenomenally. Between 1939 and 1943 the expenditures for food jumped 74 per cent, for clothing 78 per cent, for barber and beauty shop services 80 per cent. Money spent for alcohol and tobacco reached new highs. At the same time the money spent for education has virtually remained the same or at most has increased but a fraction.

"For the first time in the history of our country, the per cent of educational expenditures declined during a war period— a period when other expenditures were climbing," the National Education Association reports. "This astonishing fact should no longer be overlooked, nor the correction of this unfortunate condition longer delayed.

"While consumer expenditures maintain life and add to its satisfactions, such expenditures do not lay the basis for added future income. Expenditures for education are investments which increase the earning power of individuals and the total national income."

If the United States is to retain its leadership in the world, if it is to continue as a democratic land, the money spent for education will have to be increased. A democracy cannot afford an illiterate electorate.

It is known that nations which provide an adequate educational program emerge as strong powers, while those that neglect the education of their people fall behind in almost every respect. Perhaps that is why Russia, reading the lessons of history, is putting so much of its money and energy into education.

Money spent for education will bring back dividends many times over. It will serve as an insurance against national disaster in time of war, and will help make prosperity greater in time of peace. Although the United States has the best and freest school system in the world, it cannot sit back complacently and hope to retain its position in world leadership without a continuous and energetic effort. Although this country has more high school and college graduates than any other nation, at the same time we have more criminals, more institutions for the mentally sick, and more juvenile delinquents.

Not until America's ten million illiterates—men and women who cannot read or write—are made useful citizens can we sit back contentedly. Not until our educational expenditures equal the money we spend for liquor, cigarettes, or cosmetics can we rest on our laurels. That there is a grave danger to a democracy in an illiterate populace is evident. The influence, potential or real, of the uneducated voter cannot be lightly dismissed. The National Education Association makes this pertinent observation: during the decade of 1920-30 there were nearly three times as many persons of voting age who had not finished the sixth grade as the pluralities of the winning candidates for the presidency during those years.

We saw during the days of Selective Service, when America's man power was put to the test, how ruinous a large illiterate population can be. More than one million men were rejected for educational or mental deficiencies by the Army. Among those who registered in the draft 350,000 could not sign their names and had to resort to a mark. Tens of thousands of men were rejected because of physical unfitness. A sound educational program, placing emphasis upon physical as well as mental growth, could have reduced this number.

In several of our states one-third of the adult population have not completed more than four years of school! To expect a fourth-grade mind to judge accurately or even vote intelligently on some of the major issues of the day is to expect the impossible. It is not difficult to see a correlation between the number of persons educated in a state and the type of men it sends to Congress, the attitude it takes on national or international questions, or the way it conducts its internal affairs.

This table, showing the percentage of adults over twenty-five years of age who had not completed more than four years of school (based on the 1940 census), is significant and fraught with warning:

Louisiana	35.7	Michigan	10.2
South Carolina	34.7	Massachusetts	10.1
Mississippi	30.2	Illinois	9.6
Georgia	30.1	Wisconsin	9.4
Alabama	28.9	Colorado	9.0
New Mexico	27.3	Nevada	8.8
North Carolina	26.2	Ohio	8.4
Virginia	23.2	District of Columbia	8.2
Arkansas	23.1	New Hampshire	8.1
Tennessee	21.7	California	8.1
Kentucky	20.2	Indiana	7.7
Arizona	19.4	Minnesota	7.5
Texas	18.8	Maine	7.4
Florida	18.5	Montana	7.4
West Virginia	16.5	South Dakota	7.2
Maryland	15.3	Wyoming	7.1
Rhode Island	13.7	Vermont	6.1
Oklahoma	13.5	Kansas	6.1
Delaware	12.9	Nebraska	6.0
Pennsylvania	12.3	Washington	5.9
New York	12.1	Utah	5.5
New Jersey	12.0	Idaho	5.2
Connecticut	11.2	Oregon	5.2
North Dakota	10.8	Iowa	4.1
Missouri	10.3		

The percentage for the nation as a whole is 13.57. This is certainly a record of which most Americans will not want to boast. Among the United States population of twenty-five years and over, the median of school years completed in 1940 was 8.4.

It has gone up slightly since then, and probably will reach the
ninth year of schooling. Here is the breakdown:

		PERCENTAGE OF
AMOUNT	NUMBER	POPULATION
No schooling	2,799,923	3.8
1-4 years' schooling	7,304,689	9.9
5-6 years' schooling	8,515,111	11.6
7-8 years' schooling	25,897,953	35.1
High school		
1-3 years	11,181,995	15.2
4 years	10,551,680	14.3
College		
1-3 years	4,750,184	5.5
4 years or more	4,407,331	4.6

It is difficult to see how a citizen with less than a sixth-grade
schooling can decide on important issues, as he is called upon
to do in a democracy—yet 18,000,000 voters or potential voters
have not gone beyond the sixth grade.

Although money is not the answer to every issue, most of
our problems in education could be helped through greater
expenditures. The Army, through its experimental schools,
showed that adults can be taught to read and write in a re-
markably short period of time. Some of the men were given
the equivalent of a fourth-grade education in less than four
months. Were money available, our public schools could be
thrown open to the adults, illiterate as well as literate, so that
education could become a continuing adventure in the lives
of all men and women of this land. This would be a step
toward the training of men and women for good citizenship
and more intelligent participation in our democratic traditions.

Money spent for education is as important as money spent
for the Army, Navy, or any one of our defense units. Education
is the first line of our national defense. A properly educated
electorate is the best insurance this country has that it will

continue to flourish. We cannot prosper if we permit our schools to starve. Educators are agreed that more funds for our schools are essential.

A democratic nation deserves the best-educated electorate that money can buy.

NEVER before has the morale of the teaching staff in this country been so low as it is today. Teachers are discontented, dissatisfied with their profession, almost ashamed of being teachers.

A sampling of 1,500 typical classroom leaders and school heads throughout the nation shows a sharp decline in teacher morale. They were asked: What is your impression of teacher morale in your district today as compared with 1940-41? Fifty per cent answered that it is worse; 24 per cent said it was about the same, and 26 per cent said it was better. The same question, asked of 450 town and city superintendents, showed an even greater number who said that teacher morale was worse than it was before the war. Fifty-four per cent answered that it was worse, 23 per cent that it was about the same, and 23 per cent that it was better.

Teachers are not convinced that their profession is valuable. They no longer feel that they should serve for the benefit of mankind. They are asking: What is there in it for me? Thirty-six per cent of the classroom leaders of the nation, or more than one-third of the total number, said that they would not advise young people to undertake teaching as a lifework!

Many were bitter in their comments. A woman president of a village teachers' association in California observed: "I most certainly would not advise anyone to go into teaching. Teachers are definitely not respected as they should be by parents or students."

An elementary school principal, president of his county association in Colorado, said: "I'm advising all capable youngsters to keep out of teaching. There are other professions and occupations that are more attractive for young people to enter and in which they can make a decent living."

The president of a teachers' association in Vermont stated bluntly: "I would not advise young people to undertake teaching as a lifework until working conditions change and salaries rise materially."

The president of a large city teachers' association in Alabama observed: "I feel that it is unwise for any young person to spend five years in college preparing for a profession that does not average a living wage. America apparently puts a low value on education."

In Oregon, the principal of a high school in a large city, emphasizing that he would not recommend teaching to young people, remarked:

"Not until teachers are given the same freedom in their methods and habits of living as other people will I recommend teaching as a profession. And not until salaries are made more attractive."

Typical of those who oppose teaching, the president of a small-town teachers' organization in Massachusetts had this to say:

"I cannot recommend or advise young people to go into teaching. If I had my choice of professions I certainly wouldn't take up teaching for my life's work. I plan to change into a position that has no strings attached. During the war students were making more money than teachers. Now teachers can hardly get along and must still be the model leaders who dress fashionably, attend all local functions, and give to all charity funds."

Not all teachers feel that way, of course. Some agree with the high school English teacher in Cincinnati who declared: "Teaching is a challenge if one has faith, health, and vigor. It's the grandest work in the world."

In a small town in Washington a teacher expressed this sentiment:

"I would advise young people to undertake teaching as a life-work. The outlook for democracy in the United States is little short of tragic unless drastic measures are taken immediately to make teaching more attractive, and the depleted ranks of the teaching profession are filled by new teachers. Democracy cannot function well without educated citizens, and citizens cannot become well educated without the best teachers the nation can provide. We must guide our most promising students toward teaching."

Unfortunately, the teachers, for the most part, are too busy fighting for their salary increases to be as much concerned with democratic ideals as they might like. Even those teachers who would advise bright young scholars to enter the profession, all too frequently do it with reservations. They would so advise, they say, if salaries were raised or if the community took a greater interest in their problems.

It would appear, though, that the public is becoming aware of teachers' problems. Both the school superintendents and the teachers reported that the public's attitude toward teachers is better today than it was in 1940-41. Sixty-five per cent of the superintendents said that the public's attitude was better, 28 per cent thought it was just about the same, and 7 per cent said it was worse.

Of the teachers, 57 per cent said it was better, 37 per cent said it was the same, and 6 per cent stated it was worse. Both groups agree that the public is beginning to have a better understanding of the teachers' troubles than before the war.

Evidence of the improved public attitude can be seen in the increased salary schedules that have been adopted in many communities throughout the country. It is also evident in the support that teachers are now receiving through newspaper editorials, in magazines, and over the radio. Unfortunately, though, this support is of the "too little and too late" variety.

The teachers feel that they are the neglected citizens of the community.

This resentment is shown in various ways. One of the most important results has been the growing number of teachers who are joining the teachers' unions. Before the war unionism did not make any noticeable headway in the teaching profession. The American Federation of Teachers had an estimated 25,000 members. The C.I.O. affiliate had no strength of any kind outside of New York City.

American Federation of Teachers officials report that they have made unprecedented gains during the last two or three years. Local chapters are now found in all of the twenty-five largest cities in the United States with the exception of Houston, Texas.

"We claim the largest voluntary membership of teachers in the United States," Irvin R. Kuenzli, secretary-treasurer of the Federation, asserts. "The National Education Association membership is largely enforced."

Teachers are now joining the labor-affiliated unions in larger numbers than ever before. They have found the unions to be more effective in getting results—and they are beginning to lose faith in the slow process of waiting for the communities to provide them with the money that they feel should be theirs.

"The lack of trade-unionism in the teaching profession has been a major cause of the present crisis," Mr. Kuenzli observes. "If the teachers are not paid sufficient salaries they are going to be up in arms. There never has been so much interest in teacher unionism as there is today. We have never seen anything like it."

While the American Federation of Labor group is growing steadily stronger, the C.I.O. affiliate, although still weak throughout the country, has gained members in New York City. It now claims a total of 7,000 teachers in this city, or about 25 per cent of the teacher strength. Beyond the metropolitan area it is making little headway, although it claims to have chartered between fifteen and twenty locals during the 1946-47 school year.

Between the American Federation of Teachers and the C.I.O. there are probably 65,000 teachers in the labor unions. Never before in American history has there been such a large and growing number of teachers in the unions. They find in present conditions the need for unionism as a morale builder.

But the teachers, sometimes apologetically, insist that unless they join unions they will not get anywhere. Even though the teachers' morale has sagged dangerously, and although they join unions in search of security, they are far from radical or communistic. Lately teachers have been charged with being "reds" or tinged with pink; they have been accused of teaching un-American doctrines and of belonging to subversive groups.

School superintendents, teachers, and state commissioners were asked to estimate the percentage of teachers in their areas belonging to subversive groups or associated with such activities. Almost without exception, educators in every part of the country—East, West, North, and South—declared that few if any teachers were advocating un-American doctrines or were connected with subversive organizations. More than 98 per cent said no teachers belonged to Fascist or Communist groups. Such overwhelming testimony would indicate that the issue of communism in the classroom is exaggerated.

It is evident, however, that unless the morale of the teaching profession is raised the crisis in the nation's schools will grow worse. It is also foreseeable that if the schools continue to deteriorate, more and more teachers will join unions or go on strike. America's schoolteachers, their morale lowered, are not happy. That is why so many of them have walked out of the classrooms.

And that is why a school principal reported: "Five of my top teachers came back from service recently. Not one of them took his job in the system. One went to the Ford Motor Company, doing personnel work; one is with the Veterans Administration; the third is a salesman for a medical concern; the fourth went back to Germany with the civilian administration; and the fifth went into business with his father-in-law.

"One by one they came to me and apologized for leaving the system. They told me that they had gotten married and couldn't live on the $1,600 a year we were paying. All of them said teaching was still their first love. Someday they hoped to come back. But, of course, they never will. We can't compete with industry. The morale of my whole teaching staff is shattered."

Teacher morale is bad not only because of low pay but because of poor working conditions. Tens of thousands of classes are overcrowded. Teachers are required to do double duty, both in the classroom and in extracurricular tasks. It is difficult to get substitutes—so the regular teacher takes over the additional load. Everyone calls upon the teachers to pitch in and help, but when the pay checks come around, so the teachers say, they are quickly forgotten.

"I wouldn't mind working so hard," one of them told me, "if we got any kind of appreciation for it. But no, we don't get a word of thanks."

A prominent national educator summed up the case for the teachers when he observed: "Conditions are getting steadily worse. More pressures are constantly being placed upon the teachers. Their class loads are increasing and school supplies are dwindling. Evidently the community doesn't recognize the importance of good schools and of good teachers. The public school system is the cornerstone of our democracy. Why can't we treat the teachers as though they were the guardians of our democratic traditions?"

Working under adverse conditions can break the teachers' morale just as surely as low salaries. Many of the teachers serve in firetraps, ugly and barren.

"When I went to college," said a rural teacher in the Middle West, "my education professor urged us to teach children to appreciate beauty. But how can we? This dingy, dreary rattrap just can't be made beautiful."

"When it's cloudy we strain our eyes or wait until a little more sunlight comes in," another teacher told me. "If we had electric lights, we could do much more work."

Detroit is an example of a large city where the morale of the teachers is low, and where rumblings and grumblings have been heard for a long time. Several strike votes were taken during 1947, and repeated conferences were held between the teachers and the administration to avert a walkout. The Detroit public schools have 3,000 children housed in buildings more than fifty years old and 10,000 additional children housed in buildings more than forty years old. The city's 321 school buildings include seventy wooden shacks originally designed as temporary buildings with a use expectancy of ten years. Many of these buildings have already served for more than a quarter of a century and are still in use.

Demands for school housing facilities to serve the new populated areas of the city are the number-one problem of the Detroit board of education. Detroit's building problems are of such magnitude that their solution seems almost impossible at the moment. In 1935 building costs averaged $8,000 a room. By 1947 the costs had jumped to $31,000 a room. Some elementary school children are transported as far as twenty-four miles a day at board of education expense.

The size of classes has grown enormously. There are 1,000 elementary classes and a similar number of high school classes that contain forty or more pupils. The junior high schools have 1,680 classes with more than forty children each. Fifty per cent of the high school students—25,000 out of the 50,000—go to school on double sessions. One group meets in the morning, the other in the afternoon. Again, the building shortage prevents any improvement of this condition for years ahead. It would cost $40,000,000 to bring Detroit's buildings up to par. In the meantime, the teachers are faced with an impossible situation. They have large classes, poor equipment, inadequate supplies, and overcrowded, antiquated buildings with which to contend. Detroit estimates that it needs an additional 900 teachers to help solve the problem.

What was found in Detroit can be duplicated in numerous other towns and cities throughout the United States. The teachers face a double task—that of getting improved conditions for themselves and that of helping to raise the general standards of the school system.

Many teachers complain that they are not part of the school program; they do not get an opportunity to help formulate programs or policies. They complain that the school superintendent, principal, or supervisor makes the decisions. If they don't follow orders implicitly they are reprimanded. Teachers want to be consulted, not harassed, by administrators or supervisors. They want to feel that they are taking part in an over-all program.

Dr. J. Paul Leonard, president of San Francisco State College, made a study of fifty teachers in a medium-sized California school system to see how the program could be improved and the morale of the teachers raised. His findings are illuminating.

"Do you have individual freedom in the classroom?" Dr. Leonard asked the teachers.

"Yes, we have all the freedom in the world," they replied.

"Do you like it?" Dr. Leonard continued.

"No, we do not," came the unexpected reply.

"What do you want instead?" the president asked.

"We want some part in the educational program of the city," they answered. "Nobody consults us about the over-all setup here. There is no teamwork. So far as we know there is no established policy of any kind. The only thing we do is come to school in the morning and teach our courses from textbooks; and we don't like it."

"I thought teachers wanted to be left alone," Dr. Leonard persisted.

"No, we don't want to be left alone," they said. "We want to be brought in as a participating part of the school system. We want to tie in with the program so that we can see what happens and why. We don't want to be free and completely independent of school responsibilities. We are not happy this way. Nobody cares what we do."

Thereupon Dr. Leonard talked to six junior high school principals in the city.

"Do you have freedom in the running of your school?" he asked each one.

"Yes, we do," came the answer.

"How are the junior high schools organized here?" Dr. Leonard asked.

"We don't know," they replied. "We have complete freedom in our own individual schools, but we are not consulted as far as the city-wide program is concerned."

In his study Dr. Leonard found one principal who said he was satisfied with this arrangement. Upon investigation, he proved to be a personal friend of the superintendent of schools. On frequent occasions the superintendent would call him up and say: "Bill, what do you think of this? How would you do that?" Because he was consulted, he felt a greater interest in his work. He was drawn into the school system, and as a result he took a more active part in the school program.

Educators agree that if the morale of the teachers and supervisors is to be improved—in fact, the morale of the entire educational staff—it will be necessary to give them a feeling of participation, of active co-operation. Teachers complain that at present they are ignored; their counsel, even when asked, is hurriedly passed over.

This point was brought home to me forcefully when I spoke to an alert young woman teacher in a New Orleans public school. She had been in the system for eight years. She was a graduate of Tulane University and held also a master's degree from Louisiana State University. When I walked into her room she was surrounded by forty happy-looking first-grade children. You could tell that the six-year-olds adored her.

"Do you like your work?" I asked her.

"Yes, I do," came the quick reply. "I like teaching. I hope I can afford to stick to it. Sometimes, though, I'm about ready to quit."

"Not enough money?" I queried.

"No, it is more than that," she said. "I don't feel as though I'm part of the school program. Sure, I teach my pupils, give them the best I know how, but beyond that, what am I? I'm never consulted about the bigger school issues. I have nothing to say about the planning of the school program. Nor am I alone in feeling this way. Many of the other teachers, particularly the younger ones, talk the same way. We don't think that there is enough democratic co-operation between the teachers and the administrative staff or the school heads."

The teacher looked around at her youngsters, answered one or two persistent questions, patted a worried lad on the head reassuringly, then continued:

"Take the matter of planning the buildings. This is a comparatively new building. But does it meet the needs of the teachers? No! Now, if I had been asked to help plan the first-grade room, I certainly would not have planned it this way. I would like to have a playroom in my first grade. We shouldn't have the bulletin board way up in the sky—how do you expect these little ones to reach it? Then there is the question of windows, of the overhead lighting, of the color scheme for the walls. Little things? Yes. But important to us teachers. We have to stay with the children all day long—why can't we be consulted before a building goes up?"

I found that the complaint of the New Orleans teacher was echoed wherever I went. The teachers are anxious to become an important part of the school system. They dislike high-handed, arbitrary orders from "headquarters." Greater democratic participation in the construction of buildings, in the development of a curriculum, in the question of school discipline, in the matter of extracurricular activities, would go far toward raising teacher morale.

Sometimes the morale of the beginning teacher is strained to the breaking point. Everywhere the school officials adopt the attitude that the new teacher must undergo a term of penance. She is usually given the poorest school in the worst section of the city. She is almost always given more of the "dirty" work of the school, such as yard duty, cafeteria inspection, or various other duties that should rightfully go to a clerk.

In one western school I visited I spoke to a new teacher—she had been teaching exactly three months when I saw her. She had forty-eight children, and they were driving her haggard. These were considered the "tough" pupils, the problem cases, the children who needed special attention. In another wing of the building was an excellent, experienced teacher of twenty-four years' standing. She had eighteen children in her class—and they were the best in the school. The morale of the new teacher could easily be imagined.

"We graduated a girl from our teachers' college last term," a college president said to me. "The San Francisco schools wanted her. She was a quiet little girl but she was eager to start teaching. I know that she could become one of the top teachers in the city. But what happened? The city of San Francisco stuck her into one of the tough, underprivileged neighborhoods. In three weeks she came to my office, put her head on my desk and cried like a baby.

" 'I'm through,' she sobbed. 'I'm going to give up teaching. I can't control those children. They are bigger than I am. They use language I can't understand. This is too much for me. I'm going to get a job as a secretary in some office.' "

Whereupon the college president went to the San Francisco school officials and said: "Here's a girl you can save. She's a good teacher. But you can't keep her by sending her to that school in Third Row. She hasn't had enough experience to tackle that school. Give her ten years of experience first."

Acting on his advice, the superintendent transferred her to another school, in a more wholesome environment, with brighter children. Later the teacher came to the president and said:

"I just love teaching now. You haven't any idea how different my new school is from the one I had before. It is as though a burden had been lifted from my shoulders. I'm glad I didn't quit."

Beginning teachers are given the worst schools; they should get the best. They do not have the experience of older teachers, and there is no logical reason why a beginning teacher should carry the heavier load. It may be necessary to provide a year of internship, comparable to the hospital internship that medical graduates now get, in order to prepare the teacher to do the job expected of her. In this way her morale can be improved, and thus many a good teacher who now quits in disgust before she has found out whether she can teach, will be saved for the system.

Whether we consider the individual or the entire teaching staff of nearly one million teachers, the sad fact is that their morale has ebbed to a new low. Insufficient salaries, lack of freedom, restrictions of various sorts and an all-too-often callous attitude on the part of the community have created havoc.

If we are to build for the future, if America is to educate its boys and girls to take their rightful places in a democracy, we must look to our teachers. Continued lowering of morale may explode into violent and harmful action.

For the first time in the history of this country, schoolteachers in substantial numbers have gone out on strike or are threatening to strike. Starting with the opening of the 1946 fall term, there have been a score of major strikes involving more than 5,000 teachers and affecting 150,000 children.

Strikes are still a distinct possibility in many of the largest cities in the nation. Strike talk has been heard in Chicago, Detroit, Boston, St. Louis, New York City, and many other communities. The teachers are on the march. Even though the teachers' organizations are opposed to the use of strikes as a bargaining weapon, the classroom teacher is ready to strike. The quiet pedagogue has suddenly become vocal and militant.

Primarily the strikes have taken place or are planned because of low salaries. The stage was set when the Norwalk, Connecticut, teachers did not return to work when school reopened. After being out for eight days they won a substantial victory. A compromise agreement gave the teachers a $65,000 increase—they had asked for $90,000. This meant an annual average increase of $600 per teacher above the previous year.

Moreover, the terms of the settlement brought out the demand of the teachers for bargaining power. The Norwalk school board agreed to recognize the Norwalk Teachers Association as the bargaining agent for the teachers. The group is affiliated with the National Education Association.

The teachers refused to work because they felt that an important principle was involved. A new salary schedule had been agreed upon by representatives of the teachers, the school board, and the Norwalk Board of Estimate and Taxation. However, the Board of Estimate later refused to appropriate the total amount called for in the new schedule. The school board then drew up salary contracts adjusted to the smaller income; the school board also declined to deal with the Norwalk Teachers Association as a collective bargaining agency. As a result, when the schools reopened in September, 1946, only eight of the city's 270 teachers had signed contracts. The rest went on strike, including the daughter of Norwalk's mayor and the wife of a school board member. Technically, however, this was not a strike since the teachers were not yet under contract.

Negotiations to settle the strike ultimately involved the governor and other state officials. On the second day of the strike, Dr. Alonzo G. Grace, Connecticut state commissioner of education, announced that if the dispute were not settled locally, the state board of education would step in, employ the teachers, and operate the schools. Upholding the teachers, Dr. Grace said:

"The proposed schedule is perfectly equitable. It is a fair schedule. As a whole, teachers have been substantially underpaid for a long time."

Following the compromise settlement of the strike, and the subsequent opening of the Norwalk schools, the chairman of the professional committee of the Norwalk Teachers Association commented:

"We proved to the public that the teachers have the courage to stand for what they think is right and just."

Encouraged by the success of this strike, teachers throughout the country began to talk in terms of walkouts. For the first time, many communities found that they had to confront not one teacher, but all the teachers, in discussing working conditions. Never before had boards of education been concerned with group action on the part of teachers. It was the practice, and still is in most instances, to mail individual contracts to the teachers; the teachers either did or did not sign them. The boards would not consider conferring with the entire school staff as a body. That is, not until the strike spirit had spread the way it did during the 1946-47 school year—a year that will undoubtedly go down in school history as the period when teachers startled the complacency of the public by going out on the picket line.

In point of numbers and influence on education generally, the biggest strike took place in Buffalo the last week of February, 1947. For months the Buffalo teachers had demanded a salary increase. Elementary teachers in Buffalo were receiving from $1,775 to $2,575; the high school teachers started at $2,175 and went to $2,975. The Buffalo teachers wanted the elementary schedule to go from $2,400 to $3,600 and the high school schedule from $2,800 to $4,000. The city officials replied that the tax structure of Buffalo did not permit this increase.

Thereupon the teachers went out on strike. Oddly enough, it was the conservative Buffalo Teachers Federation, headed by an elementary school principal, that called the strike, or as the group preferred to call it, an "abstention from work." The three unions—two American Federation of Labor affiliates and one C.I.O.—did not take any active part in the plans for the strike, although they did join the other teachers in the walkout when it came. Twenty-five hundred of the three thousand Buffalo teachers walked out on a cold, windy, blustering February morning. The school system contained 72,000 pupils, and all but a handful were effectively locked out. After three days the remaining 500 teachers petitioned the school board to close the few buildings that had remained open, claiming that education in the city had become a farce. Acting on their request, all of the schools were then closed.

After one week, the city officials, the public, the teachers, and everyone else in the community had had enough. They sought a way to reopen the schools in New York State's second largest and the nation's fourteenth largest city. A compromise was reached between the mayor and the teachers—instead of the $1,025 that the teachers sought, the city promised to give them a $625 annual salary increase. Accepting this offer, the schools reopened.

In the meantime, though, the strike left many bitter scars. It divided the teachers' ranks and brought up ugly issues. I heard a teacher say bitterly as he saw a colleague pass the picket line in front of Lafayette High School:

"Did you see that rat go into the school? If any of you ever invite him to sit at our table again during luncheon I'll get up and walk out."

This did not sound like the calm dispassionate judgment one has come to expect from teachers. To these teachers, the picket line, with the snow blowing into their faces, was a new experience, entirely alien to their hitherto peaceful school existence. Yet they soon enough became adept at this task.

"We are learning something about history," an elderly teacher told me, as I stopped to chat with her. "We have been talking democracy—now we are practicing it."

"This is the first time I've ever been on a picket line," another said. "Frankly, I enjoy it. I've never been so thoroughly convinced that we are right. I'm fighting for a just cause. I'm fighting for the right to teach in our democratic schools. And I intend to stay out here until we get what we are asking for."

Couldn't they achieve their goal in any other way?

"What do you suggest?" a man of fifty-five, who had been teaching half his life, countered. "We've been trying to talk reason for the last twelve years. All we've gotten thus far has been the brush-off. I don't feel that the people of Buffalo will be awakened in any other way. I have a master's degree from Columbia University, a bachelor's from the University of Buffalo. Yet I'm supposed to get by on my $50-a-week take-home pay."

"I've always been opposed to strikes," a gray-haired Latin teacher said wistfully. "I don't think it's right to keep the children out of school. But it looks as though the city wants it this way. Aren't teachers supposed to be human beings? How long do you think we can be stepped on? It's about time that someone thought of us."

Sometimes the teachers thought beyond the matter of money. An intelligent-looking, alert teacher observed: "I'm not so much worried about my salary as I am about the state of education in Buffalo. Our schools are deteriorating rapidly. They are in poor shape. Everything is rotten here. Unless we increase salaries the city will lose its best teachers to the surrounding suburbs. The educational setup has been a political football here for years. I feel that this strike is the healthiest thing that has happened to education in our lifetime."

But this attitude did not go unchallenged. Cool heads recognized the danger that could result if the schools remained closed, and this fever spread nation-wide. The children suffered most. They ran wild through the schoolrooms, and hurled chalk as well as ugly names at their "scab" teachers. On the blackboards were written such slogans as: "We don't want you—get out and join the picket line." "Teachers are on strike for better pay—why don't you join them?" "You are a scab."

"Won't the effect of this kind of situation last with the children as well as teachers for a long time?" one of the officials wondered. "A strike is never a pleasant way to settle problems— and a teachers' strike seems even more unreasonable and unnecessary."

Serious repercussions followed the Buffalo strike. New York State passed a "no-strike" law that now prohibits teachers and other governmental employees, under pain of severe penalties, from engaging in strikes. Known as the Condon-Wadlin law— it was introduced in the state Senate by William F. Condon of Yonkers and in the Assembly by John F. Wadlin of Ulster— the measure is one of the most severe adopted in any state in the Union.

The most salient portions of the law deal with the penalties to be invoked if a teacher goes out on strike in defiance of this prohibition. A teacher may then be reappointed or re-employed only upon these conditions:

1. His compensation shall in no event exceed that received by him immediately prior to the time of such violation.
2. The compensation of such person shall not be increased until after the expiration of the three years from such appointment or reappointment, employment, or re-employment.
3. Such person shall be on probation for a period of five years following such appointment or reappointment, employment, or re-employment, during which period he shall serve without tenure and at the pleasure of the appointing officer or body.

Whether this stringent law will effectively bar strikes in New York State remains to be seen. Although the state adopted a new single-salary schedule, raising the pay of the elementary teachers, the high school teachers are not satisfied with this arrangement. They are particularly dissatisfied with the merit provision, which will keep many teachers from reaching the upper brackets of the schedule. Warning that there is no way to carry out a merit system, the teachers charge that political machinations and bootlicking will endanger the program. However, since passage of the Condon-Wadlin bill the teachers have become less vociferous. Several of the leaders have warned, though, that this bill will not keep them from striking if conditions do not improve.

"We'll just resign in a body," a spokesman said, "and then go out on strike. The law says nothing against our resigning. How would the city be able to replace 30,000 teachers?"

The Buffalo strike was not the only major school stoppage that occurred during the eventful 1946-47 school year. St. Paul, Minnesota, had a lengthy strike, lasting a full month. The strike began on November 24, 1946, when the 1,160 teachers, represented by the Teachers Joint Council, did not report to their classrooms. They demanded that their salary schedule, ranging from $1,200 to $2,600, be raised. In addition, they wanted an immediate $200 bonus.

For more than a month the strike continued, while 36,000 children stayed at home. Efforts at compromise failed; the teachers held fast. With placards the teachers picketed the schools, asking for "living wages" and describing the city's schools as "antique." Pleading an inability to meet the teachers' demands—which were for a $2,400 to $5,000 annual pay schedule—the city councilmen of St. Paul pointed to the charter limitation on city expenditure of $30 per capita as a bar. During the Christmas vacation a temporary truce was arranged, and the children returned to school.

Upon the intervention of the Trades and Labor Assembly of St. Paul, the city council agreed to recommend to the Charter Commission a charter amendment, to finance the negotiated program for school betterment. It introduced a revised salary schedule to be made effective as soon as legally proper, but to be retroactive to January 1, 1947. The schedule provided salaries ranging from $2,400 to $4,200. The Charter Commission certified the referendum for the amendment of the city charter. The strike was then suspended by the teachers to give the electorate an opportunity to vote on the amendment.

By a narrow margin the amendment was lost, and the teachers did not get their increases. The law in St. Paul requires a 60 per cent majority vote for charter amendments. The teachers received 53 per cent of the vote, the rest going against them. A vigorous campaign had been waged by both the teachers and those who opposed them, the most telling argument being that the increased salaries would add greatly to the taxes of the small home owners.

Although the teachers returned to work, they are far from satisfied. Many have threatened to resign and get jobs elsewhere. A number have already gone.

As an interesting sidelight of the St. Paul strike, the teachers not only demanded more money for themselves, but they urged an expenditure for school improvements. In a special statement, which they called the "St. Paul Story," the teachers presented a graphic picture of what they deemed essential for the

improvement of public school education in their city. The
statement read:

PICTURE A CITY—

Where many children meet in school buildings that have long been
    condemned as fire and health hazards.
Where in one of the larger elementary schools there is only one
    lavatory for boys and one for girls.
Where as many as forty-seven to fifty children meet in rooms in-
    tended for only thirty-five, so that some have been known to
    suffer burns due to crowding against radiators.
Where laboratories, shops, and classrooms are without the necessary
    equipment and supplies.
Where no free textbooks are provided.
Where the budget does not provide for school libraries.
Where maps are antiquated and practically nonexistent.
Where four of the ten high schools are not accredited.
Where poor school conditions and low salaries have forced teachers
    to seek employment elsewhere, leaving classes without qualified
    teachers.
Such are the deplorable conditions in the public schools of St. Paul,
    Minnesota.

The teachers requested that the city provide $1,700,000 for
school betterment. This money would be used to improve the
special services, to buy equipment, supplies, textbooks, as well
as to rehabilitate the school buildings and playgrounds.

A threatened strike at the twin city of Minneapolis was narrowly averted when the teachers accepted a settlement offer
which will raise their basic salaries by $1,200 a year starting in
1948. During 1947 the teachers received a flat $600 payment.
New salary schedules called for this arrangement: salaries from
$2,000 to $4,200 a year for teachers with bachelor's degrees;
$2,200 to $4,400 for teachers with master's degrees; $2,400 to
$4,600 for doctor's degrees; and $2,000 to $3,800 for teachers
without degrees.

American teachers now know what it feels like to man the
picket lines. Rural schoolteachers, always considered the

most conservative and the most amenable of any, are out in front in their strike threats. Teachers at Wilkes-Barre and East Conemaugh, Pennsylvania, struck for salary increases. The school board agreed to make regular payments due them on back pay, and to consider salary increases for next year. Although a teachers' strike for a $400 annual increase failed at Rankin, Pennsylvania, the students struck briefly in sympathy. Thirty-eight schools were closed at McMinnville, Tennessee, by a strike of teachers and bus drivers. They demanded a $25-a-month increase on their salary schedule, which ranged from $89 to $150 monthly.

Schools at Shelbyville, Tennessee, struck for $25 increases. When a $200 cost-of-living bonus was rejected at Muscoda, Wisconsin, five teachers and their students took part in a one-day walkout. More successful were the 112 teachers at Uniontown, Pennsylvania, who won $400 increases after being out for a month.

A lone teacher at Sabattus, Maine, won her strike bout, too. It took only half a day, but this sixty-nine-year-old teacher won these conditions: no more janitorial work—and she is to be driven by automobile to and from school daily. The teacher had to do the janitorial work, such as stoking the stove and sweeping the floor, when a thirteen-year-old boy, who got $1 a week for this chore, resigned.

Ten schools were closed at Shamokin, Pennsylvania, when the teachers requested a $300 bonus, together with yearly salary increases. Pawtucket, Rhode Island, ordered its schools closed after the teachers had called for a strike. The school committee refused to discuss the demand for a revised salary schedule. After two days the schools reopened; the city voted a $300 increase for all city employees, including the teachers. Providence, Rhode Island, removed the threat of a strike by adopting the single-salary schedule demanded by the Providence Teachers Association; the city voted to double the $100-a-year cost-of-living bonus to its 1,700 teachers. However, the Providence teachers were not satisfied with this arrangement.

Staid New England appears to have erupted in a series of salary demands. Boston led the way in a demand for boosts ranging from $800 to $1,200 a year. The Massachusetts Teachers Federation reported that the Bay State, once among the six best in the nation in paying teachers, had dropped to twelfth place within a year. The Massachusetts state educational department reported the average pay for its 24,000 teachers and supervisors at $2,369 annually. After a series of skirmishes, which resulted in the taking of a strike vote, the Massachusetts legislature granted the Boston teachers compromise increases, amounting to about half of what they sought. Whether this will pacify the teachers is impossible to predict. It is known that the teachers are dissatisfied and are far from happy at the results of their year-long campaign.

Brookline teachers asked for a flat $600 increase; the Cambridge school committee considered increase requests amounting to $400 a year for each teacher. The teachers of Westerly, Rhode Island, sought a $300 increase and served an ultimatum on the town. Teachers in Warwick, Rhode Island, demanded a $600 increase; Barrington, Rhode Island, teachers requested $400. Overriding the town's budget committee, Lincoln, Rhode Island, taxpayers approved pay boosts of $500. Teachers and other school employees at Marlboro, Massachusetts, won a $300 yearly increase after all had signed a petition threatening to strike.

New salary schedules were adopted in Rahway, New Jersey, which provided increases up to $500 a year; the school board in Hillside, New Jersey, agreed to a $300 raise. A one-day strike proved effective at Hawthorne, New Jersey, and the teachers were granted the $600 annual increases that they sought. The 450 New Castle County, Delaware, public school teachers warned that they would consider a strike vote unless the Delaware state legislature gave them a minimum of $2,400 a year.

Teachers closed down the grade and high school at Johnstown, Pennsylvania, when the entire staff of thirty-nine instructors struck in demand for a $300-a-year salary increase.

At Paterson, New Jersey, 545 of the 703 teachers observed a day of "illness" as a protest against the city's refusal to grant a $400 cost-of-living bonus.

A strike was narrowly averted at Dayton, Ohio. Before peace was restored, however, the superintendent of schools and the vice-president of the board had resigned. The trouble began when Local 921, American Federation of Teachers, chartered in the fall of 1946, demanded that it be recognized as a bargaining agency. The Dayton Classroom Teachers Association, an independent group, voted to approve the salary scale that the superintendent had prepared. The union opposed it.

All during the war the Dayton teachers tried unsuccessfully to get wage increases. The 1,072 teachers received annual average wages of $1,858. The district voters approved a 1½-mill levy for increasing wages. The superintendent drew up a schedule based on length of experience and college degrees. The teachers' union charged that the new program would increase the average high school teacher's pay by only $6.04 annually. A new schedule, offered by the union, was rejected by the board of education on the ground that it would cost an additional $579,000.

As an added complication, the superintendent, with the Dayton school system for thirty-one years, expressed opposition to board bargaining with the American Federation of Teachers. He said that if his salary schedule was not adopted he would resign. This he did when the board did not accept his proposals. The school board then agreed to negotiate with the American Federation of Teachers and the classroom teachers' association. While there is still some threat of strike if cost-of-living increases are not met, it is fairly certain that an agreement will be reached.

Considerable criticism of the teachers was voiced in the Dayton newspapers; some parent-teachers' association groups and business leaders warned against the strike. At the same time most of these individuals and organizations agreed that the teachers should receive wage boosts. This appears to be the generally recognized pattern followed in almost every community where the teachers have gone out on strike, or where such a strike begins to appear imminent. While siding with the teachers for more money, in most instances the community is vigorously opposed to the use of the strike weapon for teachers.

While these, and a number of other strikes and unprecedented strike threats have been sweeping the country, the school leaders have been trying to stem overt action on the part of the teachers. The amazing spectacle is presented of classroom teachers' becoming more aggressive than their own organizations. In the past teachers were reluctant to talk openly, preferring to have their organizations speak in their behalf. Today the situation has drastically changed. The St. Paul strike was instigated by an American Federation of Teachers affiliate, yet the federation has a no-strike clause in its charter. If the executive committee of the federation had so desired, it could have ousted the local for its action. But the national body did not take this drastic step. Instead, it condoned the strike on the ground that extenuating circumstances made it necessary. Similarly, no action was taken by the federation against the Pawtucket, Rhode Island, union strikers, or against those who participated in school stoppages in other cities.

It is obvious that teacher pressure may force the federation to change its no-strike policy. The State Federation of Teachers of New Jersey adopted a resolution urging its parent body, the A. F. of T., to abolish the no-strike policy that has been in effect since the organization was founded in 1917. The resolution observed that the strike "has long been deemed the most effective weapon of labor when collective bargaining and all other methods for achieving satisfactory wages and working conditions fail."

Opposition to strikes is stressed by the National Education Association, the largest professional body of teachers in the United States, with a membership of 775,000. Even though many of its members are not living up to the parent body's injunction, the Ethics Committee of the National Education Association adopted this policy regarding strikes:

"The National Education Association Ethics Committee recommends a cost-of-living adjustment in teachers' salaries. It reaffirms its position regarding the sanctity of teachers' contracts. The Ethics Committee does not endorse breaking contracts by striking. However, the Ethics Committee warns that immediate consideration must be given to upward salary adjustments in countless communities in order to avert a wholesale withdrawal of trained teachers from the profession."

At the same time, the National Education Association urged professional group action in obtaining pay raises for teachers.

"Group action is essential today," the N.E.A. said. "The former practice where teachers individually bargained with the superintendent of schools or the board of education for their salaries is largely past."

The N.E.A. proposed that a salary committee, chosen by the entire faculty, receive full authority to represent and act for the local education association. While opposed to strikes, the N.E.A. approves the "no contract, no work" position, made popular by John L. Lewis and his coal miners.

At its annual conference in Atlantic City in the spring of 1947, the American Association of School Administrators reaffirmed the stand of the National Education Association, pledging itself to continue with the no-strike program. Yet, despite the pleading of the influential school groups, the teachers are talking strike language. And what is more disturbing, they are actually going out on the picket line.

Teachers, principals, and school superintendents are disturbed at the possible repercussions. The strikes and threats of strikes are not isolated incidents. They are symptoms of the low state to which public education has fallen. Strikes are the direct result of a neglected and pauperized school system. The problem goes deep into the very fiber of our way of life.

Educators and thoughtful laymen know that a solution must

be found. In large part, we are now reaping the whirlwind. For too many years we ignored our schools, we were niggardly in our support of educational facilities, we turned away when the teachers called for our assistance.

To seek a cure we must be aware of the nature of the disease. We must know that an underpaid teaching staff cannot do a decent job. If our democratic way of life is to continue we must keep our teachers in the classroom, not on the picket line. A closed school is the symbol of a sick democracy.

Poor working conditions, inadequate retirement laws, and weak tenure protection keep thousands of capable men and women from entering the teaching profession. At present, 360,000, or 42 per cent, of the teachers have adequate tenure. The rest are at the mercy of the school boards or the local and county superintendents.

Tenure is provided teachers in the states of Alabama, Louisiana, Maryland, Massachusetts, New Jersey, New Mexico, and Pennsylvania. In California, Kentucky, and Ohio, permanent tenure is granted in the larger districts, while the smaller communities are permitted optional law. Permanent tenure in some districts, with continuing contracts in the rest, are granted teachers in Connecticut, Illinois, Indiana, Minnesota, Missouri, Nebraska, Oregon, South Carolina, Tennessee, and Wisconsin. Michigan has a permissive law for permanent tenure dependent on the approval of the local voters.

Colorado, Florida, Georgia, Kansas, and New York provide permanent tenure in some districts, but make no provisions for teachers elsewhere throughout the state. However, New York City, with its 30,000 teachers, has a strong tenure law. After a three years' probationary period the teachers get life-long protection and can be removed for cause only. With the exception of a few rural districts, tenure is granted a majority of teachers in the state.

In two states, Mississippi and North Dakota, contracts are permitted for more than one year in some districts, but no

provisions or annual elections exist in other districts. Idaho,
New Hampshire, Rhode Island, South Dakota, Utah, Vermont, and Wyoming have no legislation covering tenure. An
annual election of the teacher to her job is required in Arizona
and Oklahoma, while contracts for more than one year are
permitted in Maine and Texas.

Continuing contracts—a plan by which the teacher is notified
each spring whether or not her contract is to be renewed—exist
in Arkansas, Delaware, Iowa, Montana, Nevada, North Carolina, Virginia, Washington, and West Virginia.

Very few teachers who have the protection of a good tenure
law are wrongly dismissed. Nation-wide, a total of 155,000, or
18 per cent, of the teachers have no legislative provisions for
tenure of any kind. Another 115,000, or 13 per cent, have un-
classified protection; 235,000, or 27 per cent, have tenure on
the continuing-contracts plan.

Tenure is a safeguard for the teacher against school or community pressures. Teachers provided with a sense of security
are thereby enabled to devote all of their energies to teaching,
with a minimum of fear concerning their own employment.

"Teacher tenure makes possible better schools for our children," the National Education Association observes. "Teachers
who are secure in their employment grow in the practice of
their profession and enter actively into the affairs of the community in which they live. Good tenure laws attract and keep
in the profession those whose abilities and personal traits best
qualify them for teaching."

In all cases where tenure exists, the teachers are required
to serve a probationary period of from one to three years. In
New York City, for example, the teacher is employed on a
year-to-year basis for the first three years. If she is rated satisfactory at the end of three years, she receives her permanent
appointment. Thereafter she can be removed for cause only,
after a hearing before the board of education.

Where tenure does not exist the teacher is insecure. The
National Education Association several years ago established

a National Commission for the Defense of Democracy through Education, to give assistance to teachers who are unjustly discharged. The commission has helped teachers in many parts of the country get back their jobs, after it was found that they were discharged because of political or other unprofessional reasons. Often, by bringing a case into the open, the teacher is reinstated without a formal investigation by the commission. However, the teachers agree that a commission, no matter how powerful, cannot take the place of adequate tenure laws.

Various instances have been cited by educational groups to show the need of tenure, both for teachers and administrators. The wife of a former school superintendent comments:

"Due to political chicanery on the part of a comparatively small group, my husband, under whose guidance a suburban school system developed in twenty years from obscurity to a place of national recognition, lost his position. Now at fifty-three, still in his prime, he is forced after thirty-three years of work as an educator to look for some other type of employment. Aside from the personal tragedy involved, the fact that so great an injustice can strike a man of his integrity, without arousing action from others in the profession, explains why chaotic conditions exist in public schools today. Acute shortage of skilled teachers, yet this ruthless treatment of educators of proved ability goes on. My husband, who has been a courageous leader, is cast off like an old shoe. . . ."

In another instance, the secretary of a classroom teachers' association took the leadership in petitioning the school board for needed reforms in the schools—a cost-of-living increase in salaries, competitive examinations for principals in filling vacancies, and a survey of teachers' salaries to be made by a disinterested agency. For her activities the teacher was transferred to another building. She has also been warned by the personnel director that unless her "health" improved she would be declared "unfit to be in the schoolroom." The teacher did not protest the transfer nor did she cease her activities in the association. However, she is decidedly worried about the charge that she is ill. That particular school board has a practice of putting teachers on half salary without previous notice for physical, mental, or any "incompetency" the board desires. At forty-five, she has been teaching in the state for twelve years. Yet there is no tenure protection in her state—and now she fears that she will be declared "ill" next school year.

"I have never been more healthy in my life," she observes ruefully. "The trouble is, I'm too healthy. If I gave up my fight to improve our school conditions the board would find me strong enough to continue in my teaching job."

A rural teacher in a southern state worked through the county teachers' association to arouse interest in better salaries for teachers, physical education for high school girls, provision of school lunchroom and manual training departments, and other school reforms. At the beginning of the school year, she was notified that her contract would not be renewed. The only explanation she received from the school board was that she was being dropped "in the interest of harmony."

Commenting on these and similar instances, the National Education Association observes: "In the midst of the worst teacher shortage in our history we are actually discouraging and driving out of the profession some of our most effective teachers, the very ones in many cases who dare to speak out for school reform. To drive out these leaders is an incalculable loss to our schools. Strong tenure laws that protect all our teachers is the most powerful defense that teachers can develop."

In addition to tenure, teachers want adequate retirement laws and other forms of professional security. Some form of retirement or disability security is now in effect in almost every part of the country. Thirty-nine states have teacher-retirement or pension systems. In addition, the important cities in twenty-seven states have established local retirement systems. Although the provisions of the retirement systems vary considerably, the teachers say that on the whole this protection is far from adequate. A number of systems do not offer the teachers more than $600 a year. A plan that gives the teacher, when she reaches the age of seventy, not more than $10 to $15 a week cannot help to build professional morale. Retirement benefits range from less than $300 to $1,500 a year, with the average only about $800. In most systems the teacher and the school contribute to the fund.

Other factors combine to keep prospective teachers out of the schools. In many states the teachers do not get reasonable sick-leave provisions; in still others, maternity leaves are grudgingly granted, and then without pay. Too often teachers have little to say about their classroom assignments or where they are to be transferred. The teachers are told what to do, and are then expected to do it meekly and quietly.

One of the most common complaints by teachers that I encountered is that their lives are circumscribed by the community. This is particularly true in rural areas, although city school systems are guilty, too. Teachers all too often must be the very model of a model major general. In many communities they are not permitted to smoke, drink, dance, go out on dates, be seen in night clubs, or do anything that would cause the better citizens to frown in disapproval. Men and women will not go into teaching so long as they feel that they will be treated shabbily and not as human beings. Many communities restrict their freedom. They are told what church to attend, how to spend their evenings, what clothes to wear.

"I would suggest that you go to Main church," a teacher in a western state was told before she signed her contract.

"Why?" the teacher asked in some surprise.

"Because the members of the board of education go there," the superintendent replied frankly. "They wouldn't like it if you went someplace else."

The teacher pondered a moment and said: "But I hadn't intended to go to any church at the moment. I want to get acquainted with the community before I decide how to spend my Sundays."

"I'm awfully sorry," the superintendent said firmly. "Even

though we need a teacher with your experience, I'm afraid you're not the type that would fit into our school system."

Fifteen per cent of a representative sampling of all the teachers of the country are forbidden to smoke in public. This would mean that about 125,000 teachers are denied the right that every other member of the community now has, regardless of profession. A far greater number than that—estimated at close to 40 per cent—are forbidden to drink. The teachers indicate that even being seen with a highball in one's hand at a respectable cocktail party given by the mayor's wife, would mean dismissal as an "undesirable character." For 3 per cent, or 25,000 teachers, even the right or pleasure to dance is forbidden. They report that dancing is considered unwomanly or even sinful, and being seen on a dance floor is tantamount to giving up their teaching license.

Even where the restrictions are not specified, the teachers are aware of the forbidden zones. As the president of a teachers' education association in Minnesota observes: "Although our district is pretty liberal, most teachers remain far enough within bounds to be on the safe side."

Sometimes the teachers have become so used to their second-rate status that they accept their restrictions without protest. The president of a Kansas teachers' association observes: "Teachers have quite a lot of freedom here. However, married women cannot teach on regular salary; nor do the teachers, male or female, smoke or dance in public."

In large cities the complaints of the teachers are not so much that they cannot smoke, drink, or dance, but that they are treated as a class apart. They want to win the respect and confidence of the public. Too often the public shuns them; they become lonely outcasts.

"The teacher is not recognized as an asset in our community," a principal protests. "She is seldom appointed to any of the civic, municipal, or social committees. Teachers are segregated into a special class. We do not have the respect accorded to a minister or the freedom granted to a carpenter."

If a teacher should have the audacity to fall in love and get married, in many communities she is immediately ousted. Despite the teacher shortage, married women are not hired as full-time regular teachers in nearly one-third of the school systems of the country. If a teacher marries while she is in service, she is either discharged at once or ousted at the end of the school term. Married teachers are unwanted both in rural districts and in city school systems. In 1941 married women were refused regular positions in 58 per cent of the city schools, and were appointed under special arrangements in 29 per cent of the others. Educators are increasingly convinced that discrimination against married teachers is not only unjust but harmful to the welfare of the children.

As a result of these restrictions, the typical teacher is regarded as a spinster, a drab old maid who has lost touch with life. Teachers are not expected to be warm and human; they are bullied and must conform to the pattern set by the community. To show any independence frequently means dismissal from the profession. Yet, while on the one hand the teacher is subjected to restrictions, on the other hand she is rapidly becoming the target of pressure groups. Her academic freedom as well as personal freedom are hampered by the action of parents, school board members, administrative officials, fraternal organizations, patriotic societies, or church groups.

Lately there has been an increase in the witch-hunting that took place after World War I. Blanket charges against the teachers have been heard on many sides. They have been accused of disloyalty, of communism, of radicalism, of plots to undermine the American form of government, and of using subversive textbooks. An investigation of "pink teachers" has been promised by Representative John E. Rankin of Mississippi, member of the House Committee on un-American Activities. Mr. Rankin called upon veterans' organizations and civic groups to "drive from our educational institutions those pink professors who are now being subsidized from questionable sources."

"We are determined that this government shall not be undermined," Mr. Rankin said. "We are determined that the American government and the American way of life shall not be destroyed."

Answering this and similar charges, the National Education Association declared:

"The National Education Association represents through its active associate members over 900,000 American teachers who are thoroughly patriotic and devoted to the protection of American ideals and liberties. . . . To the best of our information there are less than 200 communists teaching in American schools. This constitutes less than two-hundredths of one per cent . . . no professional or occupational group in the entire United States is as free from subversive elements, as devoted to the principles of democracy, or as determined to safeguard our democratic futures, as the teaching profession."

One direct effect of this incessant hue and cry against "pink" or "red" teachers has been that many bright young men and women have shunned the profession. It has further lowered the already battered morale that exists among school people. As a typical teacher said:

"On the one hand we are accused of being communistic, and on the other we are asked to serve our country in its time of need. The war record of the teachers is ample proof, if more proof were needed, that we are patriotic. And the record of our students should also prove that we instilled in them the high ideals of democracy that made them ready to give their lives so that freedom might survive. We are not subversive nor do we want to overthrow our government. Why should we constantly have to protest that we are innocent? We try to serve the children in the best way we know how."

Educators are concerned at the attacks against teachers that have taken place. They are afraid that the teacher shortage, already jeopardizing the public school system, may grow worse as a result of the attacks.

Many prominent educators have urged that teachers receive a fair place in the community, that they be paid salaries commensurate with their worth. Professor Raleigh Schorling of the University of Michigan school of education has evolved a twelve-point "bill of rights" for teachers which has received commendation and support from the teaching profession. This platform includes:

1. The right to teach classes that are not too large—in general, from ten to twenty pupils.
2. The right to have time in the school day for planning.
3. The right of a 45-hour week.
4. The right to an adequate amount of helpful and constructive supervision.
5. The right to adequate compensation for the full year of fifty-two weeks.
6. The right to have good materials and enough of them.
7. The right to work in a room that, with the help of the students, can be made pleasant and appropriate to the tasks to be learned.
8. The right to the same personal liberties which other respectable citizens assume for themselves as a matter of course.
9. The right to an externship: (1) a light teaching load in the first year of teaching, perhaps half time; (2) salary appropriate to the load, ideally a living wage for a single person; (3) experience in a great variety of tasks, as, for example, extracurricular, administrative, and teaching; (4) adequate and competent supervision; (5) an opportunity to study the school and community as a whole before being limited to the teaching of a single subject or grade; (6) an arrangement truly professional which guarantees that the externship concept will not be used as a means of hiring a cheap teacher to replace a more expensive but experienced teacher; and (7) the use of gifted teachers with special interest in professional probelms to supervise beginning teachers, allowing them time in the school day to do the job and extra compensation for this valuable and technical service.
10. The right to a realistic program of in-service education.

11. The right to participate in modifying the curriculum and methods, and in formulating school policies.
12. The right to keep from being lost in the profession.

"The prospects of getting enough good teachers in the next decade are poor," Professor Schorling comments. "The fact is that many able young persons now in training, who under proper conditions would prefer to teach, are rejecting teaching as a career. It is hoped that the public may come to realize that we will never get enough good teachers, nor will the competent teachers now in service ever be able to do reasonably efficient work, until certain working conditions are improved."

These conditions must be improved before the country can get an adequate supply of competently trained teachers. Teachers are people, first and foremost. They belong to many different segments of society and cover a wide gamut of economic and social strata. When we begin to treat the teachers as human beings, we shall reap the benefits in terms of better schools, more efficient classrooms, and an educated electorate. But restrictions that hamper the teachers will have to be eliminated if the schools are to receive their quota of best minds.

ALTHOUGH the colleges and universities of this country are crowded far beyond capacity, averaging a 50 per cent increase over their peacetime high, the teachers' colleges have not made a similar comeback. During the war years the schools of education and teachers' colleges felt a drop of 50 to 75 per cent in their enrollment. Many were virtually empty.

Today they have returned to their normal registration. But they are being entered as a place of last resort by many students who cannot get in anywhere else. The teachers' colleges report that they could accommodate many more students. But the students are staying away. Teaching has lost its appeal for the young high school boy and girl. Boys, in particular, are keeping away from the teacher-training schools. They are entering other professions.

While the medical, engineering, business, law, and dental schools are flooded with applicants, the teachers' colleges are shunned. The 189 teachers' colleges of the country have an enrollment of 150,000 as compared with 143,000 in 1940. But this registration is misleading. A majority of the students do not intend to go into teaching. They have no other place to enter—and so they are attending a teachers' college, with the intention of transfer to a liberal arts college as soon as space becomes available.

By way of illustration, Pennsylvania State College found itself swamped with applicants. They could not be accommodated on the campus itself. Accordingly, 2,000 freshmen were farmed out to twenty-one other colleges in the state, mainly state teachers' colleges. Similarly, 2,500 students at the University of Minnesota were placed in the university's school of education, where they will do their first year or two of college work. After that, they will continue in the liberal arts division.

More than 1,000,000 veterans have entered colleges and universities. Another 2,000,000 have been certified as being eligible, and will enter during the next several years. But the veterans do not want the teachers' colleges. Just about 2 per cent, or 60,000, have signified their desire to go to teachers' colleges.

Both the hundred or so schools of education and the nearly 200 teachers' colleges report that they could accommodate many more students. The schools of education could accept an average of 300 more each, while the teachers' colleges have room for an average of 200 more. This condition is even more disturbing when contrasted with the liberal arts colleges. The normal 1,500,000 enrollment has gone well beyond 2,000,000, with an estimated quarter of a million qualified students turned away!

Reports from the teachers' colleges and the schools of education give the following averages per institution:

	1940-41	1946-47
TEACHERS' COLLEGES		
Men	365	568
Women	480	370
SCHOOLS OF EDUCATION		
Men	130	174
Women	257	237

The drop in women enrollments is more significant than might appear on the surface. The increase in the number of men is mainly brought about by the use of the institutions as overflow places for the regular students of the colleges or universities. Women are beginning to scorn the teachers' colleges and the teaching profession. Similarly, the veterans have indicated their dislike for teaching on numerous occasions.

During the war years the enrollment of women in teachers' colleges dropped by 40 per cent. It is still over 20 per cent less than it was in 1940. Educators are genuinely alarmed at this decline in the power of teachers' colleges to draw students.

It is true that many more men are now in the teachers' colleges than before the war. But the majority of the men are not interested in teaching. They are atending the teachers' colleges because they find it easier to gain admittance or because they have been assigned by a liberal arts college to spend their first two years there. Many colleges are using the teacher-training institutions as overflow units for their own undergraduate body.

There has been a steady decline in the relative number of students who are entering the teaching profession or who are seeking training in this area. In 1920, 22 per cent of the students in institutions of higher learning were in teachers' colleges or normal schools. By 1930 the number had dropped to 17 per cent. In 1947 only 7 per cent of the college students had enrolled in teachers' colleges. Moreover, many potential teachers, formerly trained in liberal arts colleges, are now shunning the education courses. The number of students who are preparing to teach has dropped away to a negligible handful. A recent survey by the New York State Teachers Association disclosed that only 5 per cent of high school seniors, as compared with 10 per cent in prewar years, are interested in teaching.

The reasons advanced by the high school seniors for staying away from teaching included:

1. Low wages and inadequate annual increments.
2. Little chance for advancement.

3. Inferior social position of teachers.
4. The monotony of the work.
5. Disrespectful attitude of many of the children.
6. Inability to live own life.

While the decline in potential teachers is continuing, the need for more teachers is rising. Thus, to reiterate, we are facing an increasingly acute shortage of teachers during the coming decade.

A recent study covering twenty states, made by the North Central Association of Colleges and Secondary Schools, shows that the teachers' colleges are becoming increasingly barren of students. Here are the comparisons:

In 1941, 10,182 students were completing their teaching preparation. By 1946 this number had dropped to 3,757. On the high school level, 9,327 were preparing to teach in 1941, and 4,954 in 1946. The number of teachers preparing to enter the profession decreased by 55 per cent during the past five years.

Even after they enter the teachers' colleges the percentage of those expecting to teach is much lower than it was before the war. Less than half the men in teachers' colleges today expect to teach, as compared to three-quarters of the total in 1940. Even the women show a 15 per cent decrease, while for both groups there is a 21 per cent loss.

The public attitude toward teaching may have something to do with this situation. Presidents of teachers' colleges were asked:

"In your region is teaching held in higher esteem today by the public than it was in 1940-41?"

Twenty-five per cent of the presidents said teaching was held in lower esteem. Forty per cent could not see any difference. The rest said it was higher. The same question asked of deans of schools of education brought almost identical results: 28 per cent of the deans said that teaching is held in lower esteem, 40 per cent said it was about the same, and 32 per cent thought it was higher.

Scores of college deans, presidents, professors of education, and prominent educators complain that their brightest students go into other professions. Twenty-one per cent of the teachers' college presidents said that the general ability of students entering teaching today is of poorer quality than it was in 1940. And it was poor that year!

"We have not made the teaching profession valuable enough to students to get them to enter," President Franklyn Bliss Snyder of Northwestern University points out. "Top-notch students do not go into teaching. The upper 10 per cent of students will never even think of teaching. I've been teaching and doing administrative work for twenty-five years. In all that time I have found that the ablest men and women do not enter teaching, unless as a stopgap."

"Too many of the best students are told that they are too good to go to a teachers' college," President Martin F. O'Connor of the Massachusetts State Teachers College observes.

Better students can be attracted by increasing the public regard for education and especially for the teaching profession, comments President Forrest A. Irwin of the New Jersey State Teachers College. He says: "Develop in the public mind a conviction that the teaching profession is worthy of the best equipped young people. Advance salaries to support this conviction with other professions."

Professor Raleigh Schorling of the University of Michigan, in charge of student guidance, queried the 1,288 seniors in the liberal arts college who were specializing in general science, physics, chemistry, biology, and mathematics; of the total only thirteen said that they planned to go into teaching.

"I worked with sixty-five seniors in the school of education," Professor Schorling comments. "I said to them, 'If you could get a job in some other profession, would you go into teaching?' Three of the sixty-five said they would; eight said they might.

The rest said they would not. It's a shocking situation."

The teachers themselves have very definite views as to how teaching can be improved and made more attractive. Here are a few typical comments:

A New York City teacher: "The college training courses scare potential teachers away because of excessive demands. The teacher has to be a sociologist, psychiatrist, nurse, public-relations expert, three-ring-circus director, artist, musician, etc., ad infinitum."

From a California teacher: "Emphasize the importance, the dignity, and the honor of teaching. The financial status of teachers must be more secure in order to induce able and ambitious young people to enter this most important of all fields . . . the very foundation stone of our country and the success of our way of life. I believe very definitely that more young people would go into teaching if we who are in the profession would realize the value and importance of this profession, if we were not ashamed of being teachers."

Typical, perhaps, is this terse summary from a Washington teacher: "Pay higher salaries, let teachers lead normal lives in the community, correct the impression of many people that teaching is a snap job with easy hours five days a week, nine months a year. Educate the public that teachers are normal people."

Men and women will not go into teaching as long as they feel that they will be treated shabbily. Teachers complain about the treatment they receive from the public. They complain that they are social outcasts.

"The only time I am invited to visit the home of any parent is when there is trouble with little Johnny," one teacher in Iowa said.

"The doctors and lawyers are the social pets in town," another, from Louisiana, added. "We teachers are the stepchildren."

Potential teachers are deterred from the profession because

of the community attitude as well as the attitude of the school administrators. Many have heard about the meddlesome way in which their lives are circumscribed, and will have none of it. These are the reasons most commonly listed by college men and women when they explain why they keep away from teachers' colleges: salaries are too low; teaching is dull; the teacher is not permitted to take part in preparing the school's policies; the public meddles too much with teachers' lives; teaching is nothing but a pseudoprofession; anybody can teach—you don't have to go to a teachers' college to learn.

Rightly or wrongly, these accusations influence and affect the careers that students follow. Men are refusing to enter it because they say that teaching has become a woman's profession. And the women are dropping out because they say that they are "fed up" with public scorn and ridicule.

"I'm leaving before I get that way," a teacher who had been in the system for six years said.

And another remarked: "I've been in here thirteen years and now I'm through. The children have already started to call me an old battle-ax."

Unfortunately, the majority of college students do not consider the teaching profession a good risk. Only 5 per cent consider teaching to be more desirable than the other professions, such as medicine, law, or engineering. Six hundred deans of American colleges and universities, replying to the question, "From your observations, how do your students regard entering the teaching profession as compared with other professions such as medicine, law, or engineering?" reported:

Poorer	68.3 per cent
About the same	26.7 per cent
Better	5.0 per cent

These replies include figures from women's as well as men's colleges. A still larger percentage of the deans of men reported

ing until the salary scale is raised to a level equal to that of the professions named. To expect that is to expect the impossible."

Based on the consensus of opinion of the 600 deans of liberal arts colleges and graduate schools, these are the ten most important reasons why men and women shun the teaching profession:

1. Poor salaries.
2. Community restrictions.
3. Community pressures.
4. Heavy teaching schedule.
5. Arbitrary decisions of the school administrators.
6. Too many technical regulations to obtain a teaching certificate.
7. Public attitude toward teachers as being inferior members of community.
8. Feeling among students that teaching is a field for bookworms or introverts.
9. Lack of prestige and belief that other professions offer greater community respect.
10. Political interference as a deterrent to advancement in some areas of the country, accompanied by lack of tenure and security.

Dean William C. DeVane of Yale College says: "To my regret, not many of our graduates go directly into the teaching profession, and those who do mainly wish to teach in private preparatory schools. Very few of our graduates become teachers in the public schools. Year after year, law and business—and increasingly in recent days, Washington—have attracted our all-around best graduates.

"The reasons for this neglect of public school teaching as a career are not far to seek. The public schools do not offer a very attractive career to a young man. He is impatient of the usual state requirements for a teacher's certificate. The beginning salary of a teacher is low, and the ultimate financial reward is not appropriate to the quality of mind and character required in the job."

That teachers and students consider teaching a second-rate

profession is a matter of deep concern for educators and laymen alike. In a democracy the teachers are our most valuable assets. Only when teaching receives the same respect that medicine, law, or engineering receive, will the question of how to secure better teachers be solved.

IT all depends in what part of the United States you are born whether you will get a decent education. Many sections of the country are providing totally inadequate school programs for their children. A tremendous gap exists between the good schools and the poor ones. This gap is found not only among states but within the individual state. I saw pupils going to school in hovels not fit for cattle, while a few miles away other children attended modern, up-to-date schools.

The difference in the preparation of teachers is appalling. Sixty thousand of our teachers do not have a high school education; I spoke to several who had not gone beyond the elementary grades. On the other hand, I met superior teachers, men and women with doctor of philosophy degrees and with rich educational backgrounds.

Inequalities extend to the supplies and equipment used in the schools. In a number of schools the children used battered textbooks, with little or no modern equipment of any sort. Completely lacking were the usual materials, such as paper, pencils, crayons, or maps. Yet the more favored schools had everything, complete from a library shelf to the latest science laboratories.

The type of education that a community gives its children depends on the amount of money it spends for its schools and for educational facilties. I saw at first hand ample proof to uphold the contention of Dr. Paul R. Mort, educational expert at Teachers College, Columbia University, that "money is the best single index on the quality of education."

Country-wide the national average expenditure for education in 1940 was $1,600 per classroom unit. A classroom unit represents a typical classroom in this country—with thirty children in the elementary grades and twenty-seven in the high school. Expenditure per classroom unit includes all operating expenses, such as the teacher's salary, the books and instructional supplies, as well as the expenses involved in keeping the classroom open. It does not, however, include money for new school buildings or for bus transportation. The schools show a wide gap in the amount of money they spend. Some school systems spent $6,000 a year for their classroom units, while on the further extreme, others spend as little as $100 a year. Under this latter expenditure, the teacher would get paid less than $100 annually for his services!

When the 1940 United States census was taken it was found that 20,000 children attended schools that spent $6,000 a year or more on each classroom unit; but twice as many, or 40,000, attended schools that cost less than $100 a year! The gap has widened since then. This results in a tremendous disparity in the educational opportunity offered our children. Depending upon the section of the country in which your child is born, he may have a sixty to one handicap with which to begin life.

Money is not the whole picture, although it is true that the well-financed schools provide the best teachers, the best buildings and equipment, good books, and a good curriculum. Sometimes, though, even where money is available, the schools are doing a poor job because the administration is bad. It will take a combination of both adequate funds and adequate leadership to provide the best schools for our children.

I have visited many of our poorly financed schools. Usually they have incompetent teachers, dilapidated buildings, few library books or books of any kind, and a curriculum hardly worthy of the name. Here we are back to the three R's—reading, writing, and arithmetic—with a vengeance. Yet in 1940 nearly 1,175,000 students attended classrooms that cost less than $500 a year! On the opposite extreme another 1,500,000 attended classrooms that cost more than $4,000 a year.

Unfortunately, children who need the best schools most frequently get the poorest. The better communities, where athletic fields, libraries, good playing facilities, and adequate recreational areas are available, boast the top-notch schools. But the underprivileged areas, where the children have nothing but the crowded streets in which to play and oftentimes come from drab, dull homes, find their schools even duller and drabber.

In 1940 the average classroom unit cost for the nation was $1,600. It is probably somewhat higher today, because of the increases granted to teachers. Yet the figure is accurate enough to serve as a guide. Twenty-five states fell below this classroom national average. When it is remembered that this unit includes the cost of instruction of the children together with the salary of the teacher, we must recognize that in more than half the states of the nation the average teacher gets below $1,600 annual salary. Most of these states are found in the South.

New York State, with a median expenditure per classroom unit of $4,100, leads the rest of the country; Mississippi, at the bottom of the list, spends an average of $400 for each classroom unit. Between these extremes the expenditures for the median classroom unit run as follows:

California	$3,500
New Jersey, District of Columbia	3,200
Connecticut	2,500
Massachusetts	2,400
Rhode Island, Nevada	2,300
Delaware, Washington, Illinois	2,200
Arizona, Michigan	2,100
Pennsylvania, Ohio	2,000
Wisconsin	1,900
Oregon, Wyoming	1,800

New Hampshire, Montana, Indiana, Colorado, Minnesota, Utah	1,700
Maryland, Kansas, Iowa, New Mexico	1,500
Idaho	1,400
Vermont, Texas, West Virginia, Nebraska	1,300
Florida, Louisiana, Missouri, Oklahoma, Maine	1,200
South Dakota	1,100
South Carolina	1,000
North Carolina, North Dakota	900
Virginia, Georgia, Tennessee	800
Alabama, Kentucky	700
Arkansas	500

For many, America is not a land of opportunity, Professors John K. Norton and Eugene S. Lawler write in their study *Unfinished Business in American Education*. They point to these conditions:

1. Three million adults living in the United States have never attended any kind of school.
2. Ten million adult Americans have had so little schooling that they are virtual illiterates—they cannot read and write well enough to meet the demands of modern life.
3. Half of the brightest and most talented youth of the nation leave school prematurely—before they have had the kind and amount of schooling which would be justified by both their ability and the demands of our way of life.
4. Two million children, aged six to fifteen, were not in any kind of school in 1940—and this number was substantially increased during the war.
5. The schooling provided millions of American children who are in school is so inferior and brief that it leaves them unprepared to meet the demands made upon them as citizens and as individuals.

"There can be no equal opportunity without equal educational advantages," the authors report. "In spite of exceptions, the person who leaves school prematurely feels that he is at a disadvantage. The principal reason why the public schools of America do not provide equal opportunity is that their financing is shockingly uneven. Some schools are housed in one-room shacks and taught by nearly illiterate teachers; others leave nothing to be desired in the way of spacious, comfortable, and even magnificent buildings and equipment, beauty of surroundings, and professional competence of staff. In money available between these two extremes there is a sixty to one difference."

Much is being done to bridge this gap. Despite everything, however, that has taken place, the American educational system fails to provide equal educational opportunities for the youth of the country. Vast sums of money will have to be spent by the states to improve their programs. Even to bring them to the national norm will be highly expensive.

According to *Unfinished Business in American Education,* the United States would have to spend $315,823,100 to bring those states below $1,600 up to that figure. The poorer states would have to spend much more than the more favored ones. This is what the states would be forced to spend annually, in addition to what they already allocate to schools, in order to bring all their school systems up to the national average:

Alabama	$22,645,700	Louisiana	10,006,500
Arizona	25,500	Maine	2,690,700
Arkansas	17,874,500	Maryland	1,431,700
California	84,600	Massachusetts	98,500
Colorado	1,846,000	Michigan	6,020,500
Connecticut	78,900	Minnesota	5,626,700
Delaware	47,000	Mississippi	23,284,480
Florida	6,071,100	Missouri	12,030,200
Georgia	20,872,300	Montana	1,180,600
Idaho	1,148,000	Nebraska	6,128,900
Illinois	9,222,600	Nevada	55,700
Indiana	3,236,700	New Hampshire	241,100
Iowa	8,642,700	New Jersey	108,000
Kansas	6,918,300	New Mexico	1,203,700
Kentucky	16,233,700	New York	1,818,200

North Carolina	24,780,000	Tennessee	16,918,600
North Dakota	5,324,600	Texas	16,714,900
Ohio	2,857,500	Utah	344,300
Oklahoma	8,846,800	Vermont	798,700
Oregon	1,134,200	Virginia	15,693,100
Pennsylvania	9,244,600	Washington	210,600
Rhode Island	16,500	West Virginia	5,890,700
South Carolina	11,292,700	Wisconsin	4,380,500
South Dakota	3,942,300	Wyoming	530,000

As can be seen, the greatest amounts would have to be spent by such states as Alabama, Arkansas, Florida, Georgia, Kentucky, Louisiana, Mississippi, Missouri, North and South Carolina, Oklahoma, Texas, Tennessee, and Virginia. These are the states, in the main, that would find it most difficult to increase their educational expenditures. Moreover, in these states the greatest disparities exist between the top and bottom rungs of the educational ladder.

The annual expenditure per pupil enrolled varies considerably. Nine states spent less than $50 per pupil in 1940; nine others spent more than $100 per pupil. On the bottom of the list was Mississippi—almost always found to be the "horrible example"—with an expenditure of $25 for each child; on top was New York, spending $125. A direct correlation exists between the support a state gives its schools and the number of children who attend school. In those states where education receives poor support the educational level of the whole population is low.

Sometimes inequalities exist within a state, or even within a city. For example, almost every city has its underprivileged areas. Usually the poorer sections of the city have the worst schools. This was found to be true in such typical cities as New York, Boston, Chicago, Detroit, San Francisco, New Orleans, Atlanta, and Washington. Several of the elementary schools I visited in various parts of the country were antique relics of the nineteenth century. The buildings were dilapidated; the furnishings meager; the classes overcrowded; the teachers listless and unambitious.

In one building what had been a boys' shower room—the large printed letters BOYS' SHOWER ROOM still visible on the dirty yellow door—was now an elementary classroom housing forty-seven children of the second grade. Uncovered overhead pipes made the room ugly and untidy. The room was dark and dreary; there were no curtains, no geranium plants, no bits of colored paper—not the slightest touch of beauty to brighten the lives of these youngsters.

To its credit, this room had electric lights, although they were of the dim yellowish variety and caused the children to strain their eyes to read. (A number of other schools in the country lacked even lights.) But in this room the children, on very cloudy days, had to give up reading and do something else that did not require the use of the eyes. The woman in charge, a young emergency teacher who had recently come from Oklahoma, where she had received $12 a week, tried hard. Now she was receiving $25 a week—and felt halfway human. Why did she stick to teaching?

"If you have the blood in you and are interested in children, you do not mind the pay," she said simply. "But I wish I could help these children more than I do now. It gets pretty bad here at times."

There were not enough books available—only one set of second-grade readers—eighteen of them to be spread among the forty-seven pupils. They had been read and reread, but another set was not in the offing.

"We're supposed to complete this book during the semester," the teacher explained. "We read the book the first month, and now we have three more months to go. The children are bored to death with reading the same book over and over again. Wouldn't it be nice if they could have fresh material?"

"Why not use the school library?" I asked.

"That's something we don't have in this school," she answered wistfully. "It would be heavenly if I could have another set of books for the youngsters. They're really bright, you know."

Nothing else in the way of supplies or equipment could be seen in that room. Only eight spelling books, shopworn and dog-eared, were available; these the teacher passed among the children. They could not, of course, have individual books, either for reading or for spelling. The teacher wrote the words on the board and the children copied them. Then they took the lists home and studied them as overnight homework assignments.

"It would be so much easier to teach if I had books to go around," the teacher remarked.

The small shelf in the corner of the room looked pitifully barren.

"We need arithmetic books," the teacher said. "We need art materials, crayons, paper, clay—any kind of material to give the children something to do."

In another community the school was jammed far beyond capacity. Every available inch of space was utilized; even the gymnasium became a classroom—four classrooms, in fact, with flimsy makeshift walls in between. The voices of the teachers and children carried from one room to another.

"If I just had a chance, I know that I could do a good job," the teacher, a hard-working man of fifty, said. "But what can I do here? I have nothing with which to work."

As I walked out of the school, the principal, who had accompanied me on my tour of inspection, oblivious to the appalling lack in his school, said proudly:

"Before you go, let me show you how clean we keep the corridors. They are swept every day. We never allow papers to clutter the halls."

His boasting sounded hollow to me.

The lack of a decent education for millions of American children is alarming. Under conditions that exist in many communities the children grow up in semi-ignorance; the high ideals of the teaching profession are so much rubbish.

Where does the community get the money for its schools? Part of it comes from the local unit of government, part from the state, and a negligible amount, earmarked for vocational or technical instruction, from the federal government. The amount received from the state varies from 91.7 per cent in Delaware to 4.8 per cent in Nebraska. The southern states, by and large, provide a greater percentage of the school funds to the communities than do the states in other parts of the country. On the average, the states provide 30 per cent, the federal government 2 per cent, and the local communities give the rest. This is the breakdown of state aid, as of 1945-46:

STATE	PERCENTAGE FROM STATE	STATE	PERCENTAGE FROM STATE
Alabama	68.1	Nebraska	4.8
Arizona	61.8	Nevada	17.9
Arkansas	54.9	New Hampshire	7.3
California	47.0	New Jersey	19.1
Colorado	10.7	New Mexico	76.8
Connecticut	5.9	New York	31.8
Delaware	91.7	North Carolina	63.0
Florida	44.1	North Dakota	18.6
Georgia	56.1	Ohio	43.6
Idaho	14.6	Oklahoma	44.7
Illinois	10.2	Oregon	32.2
Indiana	35.2	Pennsylvania	32.3
Iowa	15.4	Rhode Island	5.4
Kansas	20.8	South Carolina	56.1
Kentucky	39.5	South Dakota	9.8
Louisiana	58.8	Tennessee	34.9
Maine	21.5	Texas	47.8
Maryland	28.9	Utah	45.7
Massachusetts	8.7	Vermont	13.5
Michigan	40.1	Virginia	37.2
Minnesota	34.3	Washington	72.9
Mississippi	46.9	West Virginia	54.9
Missouri	35.0	Wisconsin	15.0
Montana	23.0	Wyoming	27.7

Not only inequalities between states, but inequalities within states must be eliminated if the average American boy and girl are to receive an adequate education. The slum-area schools, financed at a poverty level, have no place in a prosperous post-war America. It is essential that a minimum amount be established for all school systems, regardless of where they are found. Something more than the mere accident of birth should determine whether you and your children are to receive a sound education.

That 60 per cent of our population over twenty-five years of age have only an eighth-grade education or less is a cause for deep concern on the part of all intelligent Americans. The educational level of children and adults varies enormously among states. From 68 to 74 per cent of the adults in Georgia, Alabama, Arkansas, Tennessee, Kentucky, and West Virginia have never attended high school or college. At the same time, from 40 to 50 per cent of the adult population of Wyoming, Utah, Washington, Massachusetts, Colorado, Nevada, and California have not atended high school or college. The picture of our educational inequalities can be seen in these extremes: 35 per cent of the population over twenty-five years of age in Louisiana and South Carolina have had less than five years of schooling; only 4 per cent of the population of Iowa have had less, and 5 per cent in Idaho and Oregon.

On the question of enrollment and attendance in schools the inequalities persist in even more glaring manner. In 1940, with an average enrollment in secondary and elementary schools of 80 per cent of the population from five to nineteen years of age, Washington had an 89 per cent enrollment, Virginia 72 per cent. Washington, Utah, and Nevada had an average attendance of 152 days; Mississippi, Alabama, and Arkansas had an attendance of 123 days. Two million boys and girls, or 8 per cent of our youth within the limits of compulsory school attendance laws, were not attending school in 1940.

A similar discrepancy exists in the high school enrollments among states. In 1940, 48 per cent of the young people between fourteen and nineteen were enrolled in the public and private secondary schools of the country. Twenty-five states had an enrollment of 50 per cent or more. The highest enrollment records were made by Washington, Utah, and Nevada, with an enrollment above 60 per cent. The lowest enrollments, going below 30 per cent, were found in Mississippi, Alabama, South Carolina, Kentucky, and Arkansas. With almost repetitious monotony, the southern states are found at the bottom of every table or chart.

But the fault does not lie with these states, nor can they be condemned for neglecting the education of their children. Many of the southern states spend a greater proportion of their income for education than do the so-called wealthier states of the North or West. States with smaller per capita incomes make a greater effort to support adequate education measured by the per cent of their total income spent than do states with higher per capita incomes. They make a greater relative effort to maintain their school systems. The oft-referred-to state of Mississippi, with $30 per pupil for instruction, spends 3.2 per cent of its income. This is more than such "model" states as New York, California, New Jersey, the District of Columbia, Nevada, Ohio, or Pennsylvania spend. Louisiana, too, spends a greater proportion of its state income for public schools than does New York.

In addition to the financial gap between states, there is a wide gap in the education that children receive. Nation-wide, there are 226 children from five to seventeen years of age for each 1,000 population. In South Carolina there are 296 school-age children for each 1,000 population. In California there are only 178, and in New York 193. The southern states—Mississippi, Arkansas, Kentucky, Alabama, Tennessee, Georgia, Virginia, North Carolina, South Carolina, West Virginia, Louisiana—have a much higher ratio of school-age children to total population than the rest of the country. Someone once remarked that "where the money isn't, the children are."

What can be done to improve the situation? Educational

inequalities have been with us for many years, and it may take many more before we eliminate them. There seems to be an unbreakable cycle. The poorer states have the most children. This means that the states that can afford schools the least must put forth the greatest effort. The vast majority of children in the South receive an education that is not up to the standard of that received by children in other parts of the country. Again, it is a question of accident of birth.

In a democracy, where all children and all citizens are presumed to be equal, regardless of where they were born, unequal educational opportunities can blight our entire national well-being. Substandard schooling will mean substandard voters. Therefore, substandard schools should be a matter of grave concern not only in the South but wherever they exist. Almost every state in the Union has some substandard schools. I have seen many of them in operation. They act as cancerous growths upon the whole community, casting an ominous shadow over the everyday life of the people.

A democracy demands the full co-operation of all its citizens. It cannot afford to destroy its potential human resources, which are at once its greatest possession and its best insurance for survival. Educational inequalities stand in the way of the rich fulfillment of the democratic ideals for millions of American citizens.

TEN million American children, living in the rural areas or in farm communities, are receiving a second-class education. Even though the urban communities suffer educational problems at present, the plight of the rural schools is infinitely worse.

Thousands of one-, two- or three-room schools, found in every section of the country, are operating on standards that would not be acceptable in the most backward nations of the world. The gap between the city and rural schools, serious prior to the war, has become wider than ever before in history.

Lack of teachers is the most important cause of the rural school breakdown. In normal times the teacher frequently received her training in the rural schools. She stayed there for four or five years, and then moved on to something better. Now she doesn't stay more than a year or two. The rate of turnover in the rural schools normally is much higher than it is in the city. Today the rate of turnover has become so large that it is endangering the welfare of the children. Frequently as many as six rural teachers will come and go in one schoolroom during the course of a year. Because of the demand for teachers elsewhere, they can afford to leave their classes and enter another system, where they can get more money. Educators frankly admit that the city systems live off the "flesh and blood" of the rural schools. As a result, the rural schools are often left without teachers, or when they get teachers, they are totally unprepared to teach.

In 1940 the discrepancies between urban and rural schools was pronounced. The average length of the school term for urban areas was 182, for the rural, 168. The average salary of the instructional staff for urban schools was $37.50 a week, for rural teachers it was $18.50 weekly! Although the rural teachers have received a substantial increase over their 1940 salaries, the sum is still too low to attract or hold competent teachers. It is getting difficult to persuade even incompetent ones to remain on the job. The expense per pupil in average daily attendance for city children in 1940 was $104.72; for farm children it was $69.66. The estimated value of property per city pupil enrolled was $405; for farm children it was $185. Rural areas suffer on every count. They get teachers who are poorly trained; they lack equipment and supplies; they get little if any supervision. The rural schools, for the most part, still exemplify Whittier's well-known verse:

> Still sits the schoolhouse by the road,
> A ragged beggar sleeping.

Yet the problem of good education for all children, regardless of where they live, is important today. Americans do not stay in one place; they move about at an ever-increasing pace. During the 1930's, 14,000,000 persons moved from the farm to the cities. The migration from the southern states, where the education is the poorest, led all the rest. Twenty-two per cent of the native population of this country in 1940 lived outside the state of their birth. More than 3,000,000 living in California had been born elsewhere. More recently, under the impetus of the war years, the rate of migration assumed almost fantastic proportions. Seven out of the eleven western states boast that 50 per cent of their residents come from other states.

Obviously this interchange of citizens brings the question of educational inequality to the fore. I visited many schools, especially in what had been war-boom areas, in which the chief problem of the school officials was that of adjusting the chil-

dren who came from other cities or states to the standards of
their own communities. One teacher in a California school
complained:

"It's impossible for me to keep my class going the way it
should. I have forty-eight children, and I'm trying to do fourth-
grade work with them. Yet twelve of the children who came
from other communities evidently did not have the same type
of work that we have. They can't do the equivalent of our
second-grade work. That means that I have to devote a considerable amount of time to special lessons with them. As a
result, my other pupils suffer."

I talked with those children. They came from rural areas
where the teachers were not prepared or trained to do an adequate job in the classroom. Because of the inferior education
the rural children had received, they were under a tremendous
handicap when they moved to the city and attended well-run
schools. As this condition is today country-wide, the question
of rural versus urban education, then, is real and not academic.

Commenting on this discrepancy, the American Association
of School Administrators said in its 1945 yearbook: "In communities where the birth rate is high and where the future
citizens of the nation are growing up in disproportionately
large numbers, where the educational load is extremely heavy,
where per capita income is the lowest, where the plane of living
is far below the national average, and where cultural resources
are the most restricted, we support an inadequate educational
program although at great effort.

"American children growing up in rural areas long have
shared unequally the educational facilities provided the youth
of the nation. It is a fact of importance that for over a half
century following the Civil War the educational gains of the
nation were registered primarily in urban communities where
financial conditions were better and capacity for adaptation
greater. . . . While the city schools were obtaining more adequate financial support, drawing off from the normal schools
and colleges the best-educated teachers, enriching their in-

structional programs, providing more adequate physical facilities, and staffing themselves with trained administrative and supervisory personnel, the rural school remained much as it has been for generations."

While the urban white adults, from twenty to twenty-four years of age, attained a schooling of 12.1 years—that is, a high school education—the rural farm children had completed a median education of only 8.8 years. The differences in educational attainment of those over twenty-five years of age in the urban and rural population are striking. In almost every state persons in urban communities attained a higher education than persons in villages; it was higher in villages than among the farm population. This was true for both whites and Negroes. Especially sharp was the disparity in urban-rural education in the South.

At every occupational level from the elementary schools through the university the rural youth have a substantially poorer education than do the city children. These differences are acute in the South. While in only three southern states— Kentucky, Louisiana, and Tennessee—did the native white city population fall below the national average in median years completed, yet virtually every southern state fell below the national average in the educational attainment of the rural school areas.

Despite this poor record, the farm areas make a much greater effort to support their schools than do the urban communities. The rural areas pay a greater proportion of their per capita income, and support their schools with higher taxes, than do the urban areas. Because they do not have the money, they find it difficult, from local or state taxes, to maintain adequate schools.

At present the majority of all teachers in this country are in rural schools. Roughly, about 450,000 teachers, with 13,000,000 children, are in the rural areas. It has been estimated that at least half of these children are being taught by incompetent or inadequately prepared teachers. All of the 60,000 teachers in the country who have a high school education or less, are in the rural schools. A vast number of the 125,000 teachers under emergency certificates are also found in the rural-farm schools. Twenty-two per cent of the white and 46 per cent of the Negro teachers in one-teacher schools have attained no more than a secondary school training. Thirty-eight per cent of the one- and two-room schoolteachers had less than a two-year college education. The rural schools find it hard to attract competent teachers even in normal times, and doubly hard today during the acute teacher shortage.

According to a study made in 1943 by the United States Office of Education, 102,000 of the 140,000 public school teachers who were new to their jobs were employed in the rural schools. The following comparisons between rural and urban education, based on the 1940 United States census, are indicative of the discrepancy between rural and urban education:

The median adult between twenty and twenty-four years of age has graduated from high school; the rural adult of that age left school before he finished the first year of high school. In urban areas 97 per cent of the children thirteen years old are in elementary school, while in rural areas 91 per cent are attending. Eighty-four per cent of the sixteen-year-old urban children attend high school, while 64 per cent of the rural pupils of the same age attend.

At the same time, the adults living in villages and farms have a greater proportion of children to support. The National Resources Committee presented these figures in 1937, and they are relatively the same today:

Number of children under five years of age per 1,000 women in towns and cities, 310; in villages, 497; in rural-farm areas, 648. The number of children is greater in rural-farm than in urban areas. In the urban population of the Northeast the number of children per 1,000 women was 293; in the farm population of the southeastern states, it was 722. These high birth rates among farm districts reflect the tremendously higher educational burden that farmers must carry. Farm districts have to support a greater number of children. By way of comparison, the number of children of school age per 1,000 women in the farm population is: South Carolina, 722; Alabama, 706; New Mexico, 693; Utah, 681. The corresponding figures for cities are: California, 219; Washington, 240; Missouri, 261; Illinois, 272; New York, 282.

To complicate the problem, while the southeastern states had 13 per cent of all school-age children, the farmers in that region took in only 2 per cent of the national income. By way of contrast, the urban population of the northeastern states accounted for 42 per cent of the national income, but had to support only 27 per cent of the children of school age. This appalling disparity lies at the bottom of the poor education that rural children receive. The Brookings Institution has estimated that for each dollar of income available for the education of the farm child there was $4.44 available for the urban pupil. When we see the financial and population pattern of the farm and urban communities, it is not difficult to understand why rural youth does not have the same educational opportunity accorded to city children.

When combined with the current teacher crisis, the situation is at its deplorable worst. In many instances children are transported twenty to thirty miles a day to get to their schools. High school students are particularly hard hit. Many parts of the country do not offer their children the opportunity of attending any high school. Since none exists in his neighborhood, it often means that the child has the alternative of stopping all formal education after the elementary grades, or of leaving his home and boarding out in the nearest city where a high school exists. As this is too expensive for most parents, who are usually poor and underprivileged, the result has been that schooling is blocked for a large percentage of youth. Twenty per cent fewer farm children than city boys and girls go to high school. And the number of rural teachers who are quitting their jobs is increasing steadily in this postwar period.

Here is the breakdown of the 19,553,997 youth in the United

States between the ages of twelve and nineteen, based on United States Office of Education estimates:

> 10,106,241 live in urban communities
> 4,001,188 live in rural-nonfarm communities
> 5,446,568 live in rural-farm communities

Seventy-five per cent of the 6,500,000 boys and girls in American high schools attend schools that contain less than 300 pupils.

"The brunt of the teacher shortage is borne by the rural schools," Dr. Howard A. Dawson, director of rural education for the National Education Association, points out. "As a result of the war the rural schools have deteriorated; they have lost their best teachers. The situation is acute."

Whenever a rural school gets an outstanding teacher she is soon stolen by the near-by larger community. That experience is repeated time and again, as scores of county superintendents told me.

"We had an excellent teacher here last year," a county superintendent said. "She did a good job; she brought the parents into the school. She went to the near-by city of Chicago for books and arranged to have a traveling library come to the school. For a year the farm community had one of the best schools in the neighborhood. Then along came a high school principal and offered her more money. I just couldn't hold her, since I was paying $135 a month and he raised it to $200. This past year I've had six different teachers. They don't stick around long; I guess I get the leftovers and has-beens. Many have bad personalities. Some of them just can't teach at all.

"Right now the teacher I hired is on an emergency license. She is the whining, carping type. The parents want her ousted, but who could I put in her place? She's had a fight with the trustees, the school board, the children, and the parents. I guess I'll have to let her go, but what will I do next? She's the fourth teacher the kids have had this term. Maybe we don't pay them enough. She gets $165 a month, nine months of the year."

A visit to that school, a typical two-room country school-house, showed the extent of the demoralization that had already taken place. Forty-four children, from ages five to fifteen, sat huddled in their overcoats. Many wore mittens. It was cold outside and just as cold inside. Something had gone wrong with the furnace.

"Too many parents come in to bother and interfere with me," the teacher, a pinch-faced woman of sixty, started to whine. "I haven't taught for the last eighteen years—I don't know why I came back, except I can use the money. These kids drive me crazy. They're the worst bunch of trash in the section. The other teacher—she's causing me a lot of trouble, too. I'd like to get rid of the whole business—I don't think I'll be back after Christmas. I can get a better job in town."

"And she probably can," the superintendent said later. "That's what we're up against. The teachers are the poorest of the lot. What do we have to pick from? All the top teachers go to the school systems where they can get more money. Before the war I wouldn't have let a teacher of that kind into my office. Now I don't dare to say a word for fear she'll leave me and we'll have to close down the school."

Not all rural teachers are incompetent. I watched a number in the classroom who were excellent. One was teaching in a garage—the regular school had burned down. Twenty-seven youngsters from five to fifteen were crowded into quarters that had been built for a Ford car. Yet it was kept clean; the children were alert and responsive.

"This is my fourth year here," the teacher began. "I have a family of four myself; they've grown up and I have time to myself. I live on the farm near by. My husband died three years ago. When I took over, this school had had five teachers in three months. But I'm going to stick. The $30 a week comes in handy. I don't think that's enough, do you?"

She paused for a moment and the children waited expectantly. They had heard part of the conversation. "I like rural schoolteaching," she went on. "I guess I'm just a farmer at heart. We have lots of fun here, even though we have to make our own supplies most of the time. It's tough on some kids, walking here three miles in bad weather, but we get along. Sure, I could make more money in the big city, but I belong here with the children. Someone should stay with them."

Living conditions complicate the rural problem. Frequently the school is located in an inaccessible spot. Unless the teacher has her own automobile, it is difficult to reach the school. Yet even under these conditions some of the teachers show enthusiasm and pride in their work. A teacher applied to the county superintendent for a post in one of the backwoods areas of a midwestern state.

"You'll have to live out there," the superintendent told her.

"That is better still," came the reply. "I want to know the people. By the way, what do you expect from a rural school?"

"I have always felt that in a rural school an adult program should move simultaneously with the regular work," the superintendent answered.

"And so do I," the teacher agreed.

Whereupon she went out and organized the curriculum in a manner that had not been done before. She offered the community a sound, progressive type of school. The children reacted marvelously. She opened new worlds to them. The parent-teacher association became active and helped develop this small, two-room school. Hitherto the most exciting business of the parents had been when they discussed how to spend the $10 in the treasury. But under the inspiring guidance of the rural teacher, that changed. In many of the homes no books, with the exception of the Bible, could be found. The new teacher helped the parents secure fiction and general books; the men received books on agriculture from the school—and more to the point, they actualy sat down and read them.

"She worked hard that first year," the superintendent recalled, as we spent the afternoon at the school. "She arranged socials, musicals, and square dances. To top it off, she arranged for a series of lectures by prominent men of the community. A banker gave a talk on how to budget farm income. A newspaper editor gave a series of talks on international affairs. We brought a radio into the classroom and had our own town meeting of the air right in school.

"But I knew it couldn't last. She was too good. One of the near-by high schools heard about her, the superintendent came along, and offered her more money. I just couldn't hold her. We paid her $1,568 a year—she is now getting $2,600."

In less than a year the new teacher has destroyed everything the previous teacher had developed. "If she doesn't get her way she begins to cry," the county superintendent said. "Even though I was told that she was a problem teacher, I just couldn't get anyone else. We have to take whomever we can get."

One rural community I visited in the Far West was typical of what the war boom, together with the shortage of teachers and building supplies, has done to the rural schools. Double sessions were in effect throughout most of the schools in that district. The teacher shortage had grown until it had swept over the entire community. Thirty-five per cent of the teachers were on emergency licenses. A consolidated high school, designed for 400, was used by 2,300 students. Thirty portable shacks were added to the school, and used as classrooms. A high teacher turnover kept the system in an unstable condition.

In a fourth grade, forty-nine restless children were crowded into a room designed to hold a maximum of thirty-five. The room was dark, ugly, dreary. The children had to strain to see the blackboard; those in the rear of the room could not see it at all.

"It's awfully difficult to keep order," the teacher, a graduate of the University of California, said. "I can't give them individual attention. As a result, many are way behind in their work. The trouble is, half of the children can't see the blackboard. No matter how I arrange the room it is still bad. The walls are like shells—the passing busses simply make talking too difficult for any of us. Sometimes it's just bedlam; you can't hear yourself think.

"The children sit in seats that are either too big or too little for them. But we can't adjust the seats, as another group uses this room in the morning. My pupils have to carry their books and overcoats with them wherever they go."

She paused a moment, and then said: "If I could only have a class of thirty, with a room of my own! Wouldn't that be ideal? Last year I had fifty-two children."

The county superintendent, aware of the problems, finds that his own hands are tied. "Everyone thought that when the war ended our troubles would be over," he told me. "But they're not. Conditions are worse than ever before. There just doesn't seem any way to end our double sessions. We need more school buildings but the cost is prohibitive. I don't see any bright spot or any immediate relief. The children are not getting a square deal."

Similar conditions exist in almost every section of the country. A tour through rural schools in California disclosed dreary, overcrowded hovels used for schoolrooms. Classes were overcrowded; teachers were poorly prepared for their jobs, although in most instances enthusiastic about their work.

"Our rural schools are up against it," Dr. Vaughn D. Siedel, one of the county superintendents, remarked. "We don't have enough money nor do we know where we can get the teachers we need. We've taken women just out of high school; others have been coaxed to come out of retirement. Both types are not giving us the results we have come to expect in this day and age."

One of the schools, running on double shifts, used not only the classrooms but the auditorium and corridors. During lunch hour one section of the auditorium was used as a cafeteria, another part as a workshop, still a third was converted into a classroom. Flimsy curtains separated the different rooms. The din was beyond description. One of the teachers observed grimly that the school should be torn down, having outlived its usefulness soon after the Gold Rush.

In one of the southern states the superintendent bemoaned the lack of educational opportunities for the rural children. One of the schools had burned down five years ago but had not as yet been replaced. The children met in what had once been a cowshed. In all, 120 elementary children were attending this school, some walking five miles or more daily to reach it. There was no transportation service available.

"Where is your high school?" I asked him.

"We have no high school in this county," he explained.

"But what happens when the children leave grammar school?" I asked.

"They stop going to school," he answered. "Less than 5 per cent of our elementary children go to high school. Of every 100 children who come to us, about five go on with their schooling. They'd have to go about 150 miles to the nearest high school. Most of the farmers here are poor and can't afford that expense."

Many of the rural school buildings not only lack electric lights but they have no windows. I saw some without doors. The only light available comes in through the opening that serves as the door. On cloudy days little can be taught; on rainy days school is dismissed.

Rural schools are particularly in need of modern equipment. Many lack supplies that are ordinarily considered minimum essentials for any self-respecting school. In one typical rural high school, the only science equipment available was a map on the wall, pre-World War I model! No microscopes, no Bunsen burners, no test tubes, no laboratory equipment of any kind.

"You can't teach much science this way," the instructor, who had had twenty years of experience, admitted. "It's just a hit-and-run affair. I try to do the best I can. I guess you'd call this the horse-and-buggy way of teaching. The atomic age? We've got a long way to go before we get out of the woods. These youngsters will know very little about what is happening in the world about them when they leave here."

"Some of my children act rough and I have to do a little switching for it," an emergency schoolteacher in Georgia with less than a high school education said. "Four of the children—they are from ten to twelve years old—had never gone to school before. It's hard to start them off. But I let the older pupils work with the beginners. I turn over some of the little children to the two girls in the seventh grade. It works out all right. Things aren't too good for us. We don't have books or paper except what the kids buy themselves. I'm my own janitor and cleaner. I guess I earn my $70 a month, don't I?"

Another emergency teacher had thirty-four children in a one-room school, similar to many of the others. Three small pigs were rooting around the door, guzzling slops, but they squealed and dashed off as we approached. The teacher, a pale-looking, mousy, faded woman of about thirty, gazed at us in surprise tinged with anxiety.

"I've always loved children," she confided, when the ice had been broken. "Before I started to teach I raised my own nieces and nephews. Now I get $77.50 a month—only $68 to take home—but that helps. I'm not married so I can live at home with my parents. If it wasn't for that I couldn't manage. I didn't have a chance to finish high school but someday I'd like to go back and finish up the last two years."

It is difficult to teach so many children, handling seven grades simultaneously. It would take an experienced teacher to do an adequate job. Yet this emergency teacher was attempting to do it without guidance, without previous experience, without educational background or training of any kind beyond that received in raising her nieces and nephews.

"While I'm working with the little ones I find it difficult to keep the older ones busy," she confessed. "But I think I'll stay in teaching. This is my first year doing this kind of work. It's better than staying at home keeping house. No other work interests me."

The children giggled and whispered among themselves as I stood in front of the room and talked with their teacher. They were shy, diffident, ill at ease.

"I try not to let them upset me," she continued. "When they get temper tantrums I just leave them alone until they get over their mad spell. Then I begin teaching again. Love and kindness are better than switching. Some of the children are here for the first time. I have to start them with beginners' words. It's kind of hard to work with them. It makes the problem difficult. I guess I'll manage, though."

What about physical equipment?

"We don't have any books or a playground," she said. "The children don't get any paper except what I furnish. I have to buy paper, crayons, pencils, and things like that. It costs me four or five dollars every month, but I figure it's necessary. The county doesn't repay me for that. I'm my own janitor, too. If the children come here first they build the fire; otherwise I do. The potbellied stove isn't too good. We freeze until ten-thirty or eleven till it gets heated enough, and then we roast."

The teacher walked over to the door as we headed for the next county. "If you want to say what I'd like," she offered, "tell them I'd enjoy teaching in one grade. There are too many discipline problems with all the seven grades in one room. We're supposed to get help, but the supervisor comes about once a year. He hasn't come this year yet."

Then she said quietly, her voice filled with enthusiasm:

"I want them to be good citizens. I'm trying my best, but it's so hard with what little we got here. They deserve better."

In the adjoining county a two-room school, attended by eighty-three children, could hardly serve as an inspiration to young America. The shedlike building—unpainted, weather-beaten, drab—appeared ready to fall. It had been used for the last sixty years, and would probably serve another sixty. Inside, long benches served as both chairs and desks. Lacking electric lights, the classes could be held only on sunny days. The two windows, evidently broken some decades back, were boarded up by heavy planks. The usual potbellied stove gave off its hot and cold waves, and left the room with an eye-smarting acrid odor.

"You can't have much heart to fix up a place like this, now, can you?" the teacher asked.

The old-fashioned bucket well could have delighted a collector of early Americana. "I throw a mess of lime into the well every once in a while," the teacher said. "I hope it clears it up."

Not all rural schools are run down, anemic, or seedy. The Tallapoosa school in Georgia is an example of what a rural school can do under able guidance. A visit to the school discloses the wealth of material, the understanding, and the sympathetic approach of the teachers. While in most rural schools the youngsters are shy, diffident, awkward, and scared, at the Tallapoosa school they are active, intelligent, confident children. It is difficult to find better native poise in any well-run city school. One reason for this success, perhaps, is that the school is used as a training center of the near-by West Georgia College, where teachers are prepared for rural elementary schools. The teacher in charge of the school, a graduate of the University of Georgia, has arranged this school so that the children and the community take pride in their work. She gets complete co-operation from the college.

"I like the children and I think they like me," she remarked simply. "That is why they are so good."

The children help to plan the work of the school. On one occasion several of the pupils—there are sixty here with two teachers—shot firecrackers in school. The children got together and discussed why it was unsafe to carry on such activities in the classroom. They reached the conclusion that this was disruptive and should not be permitted. A committee of young students was appointed to supervise activities in other, more constructive directions. Moreover, the school has departed from the traditional, unrealistic curriculum found in so many rural schools, and is related more closely to the child's everyday life.

The children tell about the cattle their fathers bought, or about the way they helped plant the season's crops. In the evening the parents come to school and discuss mutual problems. Parents, children, and teachers meet frequently. This is, in every sense, a community project.

The school program goes far beyond the meager three R's. It is rich and filled with challenge and interest for the young pupils, most of whom come from underprivileged homes and all of whom lack the ordinary luxuries found in the nonrural areas. On the wall is written the general plan for the day's schedule, which reads like this:

1. Sharing time
2. Reading groups
3. Social science
4. Spelling partners
5. Arithmetic
6. Playtime games
7. Science reading
8. Lunch
9. Free choice
10. Music—art—build—sew
11. English work
12. Clean-up time
13. Story time

On the opposite blackboard are listed the health practices that the children are expected to follow:

1. Eat hot lunch
2. Play outdoors
3. Play indoor games
4. Wear raincoats
5. Wear overshoes
6. Wear rain hats
7. Keep ourselves clean
8. Keep toilets clean
9. Keep building clean
10. Help keep home clean
11. Take immunization
12. Cover cough or sneeze
13. Wash hands before we eat

The school has a definite objective—that of developing well-rounded, wholesome, intelligent citizens. Perhaps it departs from the traditional pattern, but it has caught the imagination of the pupils, the teachers, and the parents.

Another rural school that has done a magnificent job, also in Carroll County, Georgia, is the Sand Hill school. This school is also under the guidance of near-by West Georgia College. A constructive program has been established, one that has proved highly successful. In a sixth-grade class newspapers are used to supplement the textbooks. The day I visited the school the children had written on the blackboard:

We are going to look and listen for news about the following:

1. Carrollton and Carroll County
2. Georgia
3. Workers and labor unions
4. Foreign countries
5. United Nations Organization
6. Army and Navy
7. Science
8. Agriculture
9. Sports
10. Schools
11. Editorials

This consolidated school has brought together the children of the community into pleasant, highly enjoyable surroundings. The teachers appeared alert, the children were at ease, the classrooms amply supplied with modern equipment and material. Books were all about, and the children used them frequently. The modern teaching methods were abreast of any used in the best school systems of the nation. Model schools of this kind are rare to find, either in Georgia or elsewhere. Sympathetic, understanding teachers are even more difficult to meet.

It is estimated that the average school in this country is twenty-five years behind the developments made in the field of education. Old, archaic, outmoded teaching methods and procedures are still the general rule, not the exception. If the average school is twenty-five years behind new methods and practices, the rural schools are fifty years behind. Many of these Rip Van Winkles are still sleeping soundly, unaware of new developments and changes that have taken place in education and the world at large.

Probably the best rural schools can be found in New York State, where consolidation is now proceeding at a rapid pace. A number of them can serve as pilot schools for all rural education. The worst rural schools are to be found in the southeastern, the mid-western, the north central, and the New England areas, in that order.

Rural teachers are not so adequately trained as urban ones. This is true not only today but was the case before the war. Here is the condition that existed in 1937-38, a typical prewar year:

Of white urban classroom teachers—
    4 per cent had less than two years of college preparation
    36 per cent had two years but less than four
    60 per cent had four years or more
Of white rural classroom teachers—
    16 per cent had less than two years of college preparation
    44 per cent had two years but less than four
    40 per cent had four years or more

The professional experience of the teachers took this pattern:

    Teacher in one-teacher rural schools—5 years
    Two- or more-teacher rural schools—7 years
    Village under 2,500—7 years
    City 2,500 to 5,000—9 years
    City 5,000 to 10,000—11 years
    City 10,000 to 30,000—13 years
    City 30,000 to 100,000—15 years
    City over 100,000—16 years

There is a direct relationship between the size of the community and the experience and professional training of the teacher. The child who lives in a city has a better chance of getting a competent, experienced person as his teacher. Most likely the rural student will draw a teacher with far less experience or educational background than his city cousin.

With 10,000,000 children attending rural schools, and 450,000 teachers employed, it would appear necessary to develop a better system of rural education in this country. A sweeping reorganization of the entire system of rural education would give milions of American children a greater opportunity to become intelligent voters in a democratic land.

IF the American primary and secondary school system were a sixty-story skyscraper, on the top floor would be 20,000 New York school children receiving an education which costs $6,000 per classroom a year. Sixty stories down would be 38,000 Negro children in schools of Arkansas, Georgia, and Tennessee, receiving financial support of less than $100 per classroom. If a rocket bomb blew off twenty-eight stories of the skyscraper, not a single Negro child in the segregated school systems would be obliged to leave his classroom. If yet another bomb should blow away all the building except the four bottom floors, 99 per cent of the white children in the United States would have their schools destroyed, but over half of the Negro school children would be unaffected. At best they would have classrooms costing $400 per year, with a teacher whose salary would be $232 a year in Mississippi, or $371 a year in South Carolina.

The education received by Negroes in the United States is a national disgrace. A widespread disparity exists between education for Negroes and for white children. Seventeen of the southern states maintain, by state law, dual systems of education—one set of schools for the white children, another for the Negroes. Within these systems the most serious deficiencies lie. By and large all children, white or colored, receive similar treatment in all but the states where segregation exists. While it is true that in Harlem, for example, some schools attended by Negro children are not so adequately equipped as are the schools in the rest of New York City, the gap between the good and the bad is not serious.

Frequently in the dual states the Negro child does not have the opportunity to secure as thorough an education as the white pupil. His teachers are far less competent and receive substantially lower salaries. The school plants are inadequate, the equipment and supplies are usually meager and obsolete. No matter how bad the school program is in the rural white schools of the country, the situation is worse in the Negro schools. Frequently the Negro child cannot go beyond the seventh or eighth grade. In certain sections of fifteen states where 1,200,000 Negro children live there are no four-year public high schools. Out of 9,000,000 Negroes in eighteen states there are 30,000 candidates for high school graduation in a normal year.

But the situation on the higher educational level is even worse. Prior to the war the governmental units of the nation spent $192,394,548 in support of higher education; of this sum, $4,820,082 went for higher educational institutions for the Negro. While the federal and state governments contributed $92,903,750 toward the budgets of sixty-nine land-grant colleges, only $1,931,782 of this total went to the seventeen land-grant colleges for Negroes.

"Here, then, is the segregated system of Negro education," Dr. Mordecai W. Johnson, president of Howard University, observes. "It is a miserable commentary upon the health of the American democratic will. There can be no wonder that in this time of crisis the leaders of the Army have been obliged to reject 34.5 per cent of all Negro selectees on account of educational deficiencies—one state rejecting as high as 43 per cent. The system of education which we have provided for the Negro has all but butchered his children and it has crippled the nation in her most precious resources—intelligently able men."

Some of the Negro schools I visited would be a disgrace to any community. One, in particular, deserves mention. It was located about fifteen miles from the nearest village. We drove by car and had to go through tortuous, winding dirt roads that at times were all but impassable. Finally the car stopped in front of an open field. Nothing but a wooden shack, about the size of a trailer, ugly, unkempt, unpainted, could be seen. A few hogs rooted about, and several goats were nibbling at what remained of the grass stubs.

"Where is the school?" I inquired in some surprise.

"This is the school," the county superintendent, who was my guide, answered. Then he added, as we got out of the machine: "Be careful of these mud holes. Last time I stepped into mud over my ankles and had a deuce of a time getting out."

The school proved to be an old chicken coop that had not been fixed up in any way. It was a small tumble-down hovel, with a flimsy wall that went halfway to the ceiling to serve as a partition. Two classes were in session when I arrived, one on each side of the wall. About forty children were crowded into each section—they sat huddled on hard benches, made from crude slabs of wood. There were no tables or other equipment of any kind. An old potbellied stove stood in the corner, belching smoke from a cracked side. There were no windows or any lights in the shack. The teacher stood in front of the room, near the opening that served as a door. Immediately in back of the little building was an old-fashioned crude privy, built by the Negroes from odd scraps of lumber. Only one such outhouse was available, and that was used by the eighty boys and girls. During recess the boys would run into the near-by bushes and let the girls use the only means of convenience.

Not only the building, but the equipment was old and obsolete. There were not enough books to go around—the forty children had less than a dozen readers. The school did not have a blackboard, chalk, crayons, or pencils. The teacher tried the best he could to give his charges an education—but it was meager in the extreme. Crowding forty children in a space large enough for ten, and then denying them even the elementary tools of learning, had its disadvantages. On a cloudy day it was impossible to do anything more than sit around and talk. If it rained class was dismissed—the rain would sweep into the open doorway or come from the cracks in the ceiling and the walls.

An intelligent-looking Negro, a veteran of World War II, served as teacher, janitor, and truant officer rolled into one. A graduate of Southern University, he had his bachelor of science degree and had taken some work toward a master's. Eight months of the year he received $105 a month—and the other four months he worked as a gardener on one of the estates at $28 a week.

"We are very much overcrowded here," he said. "We'd like to have a building that would give us individual desks for the children and where I could get around to them better. The noise next door disturbs us. I like to teach fairly well—but it's pretty hard to get along on what I make. I have to support a wife and three children."

"What happens to these pupils after they reach the seventh grade?" I asked. "Where do they go from here?"

"They have no place to go," he replied. "Their education ends here. We do not have a high school for colored children in this county. The nearest one is nearly 200 miles away, and transportation is not provided."

It seemed hard to believe, yet here were eighty children— and their number could be multiplied many times—who had to stop when they reached the seventh grade.

But poor conditions for Negro children exist in the large cities as well as in the rural areas. One city I visited in the South had good as well as poor schools for Negroes. The good one—a technical high school—was excellent. It contained modern equipment, good workrooms, shops, and competent teachers. The school could serve as a model for the nation. But not less than a mile away from this up-to-date structure was a disreputable-looking wooden shed, which 350 children from the first through the seventh grades attended. Divided into six rooms, the school was a flimsy firetrap. The usual potbellied stove in each room roasted the children in the front rows while those in the back of the room wore their overcoats. About sixty children were crowded into each room. Although textbooks were available, no other materials were provided. Crowded two and even three to a seat, the children took their lot stoically, jostling each other when the teacher's back was turned, acting, indeed, the same as any group of normal, healthy children at that age.

"I have my bachelor's degree," one of the teachers, a middle-aged woman, said. "I've been teaching here for eighteen years—and get $98 a month for nine months of the year. This building was condemned thirty years ago—but it was turned over to the colored children. It's just a shack, a firetrap."

"This is my first year as a teacher," another one volunteered. "On cloudy days we just can't read. I have sixty-three pupils in the sixth grade. Schoolwork could be so much more interesting if only we had the right kind of supplies and materials. But we just have to make the best of it."

The principal of the school spoke up: "I would ask only for a nice clean room with suitable equipment so that the children wouldn't have to double up. If only we had lights in this building or a better heating system. When it rains the roof leaks like a sieve. We can't do any effective work that way."

These Negro teachers were not alone in their complaints. Everywhere the Negro children have a lower educational standard than the white ones. Fortunately in many parts of the South the local communities and the states are attempting to equalize educational opportunities. In the most critical period of the nation's history, when the nation was in desperate need of man power, a third of the Negroes were rejected from the armed forces for educational deficiencies. Of those who were accepted, the official War Department report on the utilization of Negro man power in the postwar Army had this to say:

"In the placement of men who were accepted, the Army encountered considerable difficulty. Leadership qualities had not been developed among the Negroes, due principally to environment and lack of opportunity. These factors had also affected their development in the various skills and crafts."

Increasing educational opportunities for Negroes between the two world wars have resulted in a greater proportion of Negroes who have the skills and training to serve their country. The Army's report points to the great strides the Negro has made in education, but a wide gap still exists between Negro— especially the southern Negro—and white pupil.

	World War I	*World War II*		
		NEGROES		
		OF 12		WHITES
	ALL	SOUTHERN	OTHER	OF THE
	NEGROES	STATES	NEGROES	U. S.
1 to 8 years grade school	95%	64%	40%	26%
1 to 4 years high school	5%	32%	53%	62%
1 or more years of college ...	few	4%	7%	12%

A far higher percentage of Negroes than white selectees were deferred because of educational deficiency. This table is indicative:

Percentage of registrants classified who were deferred because of educational deficiency, May 15, 1941-September 15, 1941

STATE	PER CENT OF WHITE	PER CENT OF NEGRO	STATE	PER CENT OF WHITE	PER CENT OF NEGRO
Alabama	1.5	8.7	Georgia	3.2	19.9
Arizona	2.6	3.6	Idaho	.2	8.6
Arkansas	3.0	15.3	Illinois	.2	1.7
California	.4	1.0	Indiana	.2	1.4
Colorado	.2	.5	Iowa	.3	.8
Connecticut	.1	1.2	Kansas	.3	1.2
Delaware	.3	3.3	Kentucky	4.4	5.4
District of			Louisiana	4.5	21.5
Columbia	.2	5.2	Maine	.7	0
Florida	1.4	17.4	Maryland	.7	11.3

STATE	PER CENT OF WHITE	PER CENT OF NEGRO	STATE	PER CENT OF WHITE	PER CENT OF NEGRO
Massachusetts	.2	.7	Oklahoma	1.5	3.7
Michigan	.3	.9	Oregon	.1	1.2
Minnesota	.5	1.2	Pennsylvania	.3	2.4
Mississippi	1.9	15.4	Rhode Island	.4	0
Missouri	.9	5.6	South Carolina ..	3.1	21.4
Montana	.2	0	South Dakota ...	.2	8.3
Nebraska	.1	.4	Tennessee	3.7	9.4
Nevada	.2	0	Texas	2.7	6.5
New Hampshire..	.4	8.7	Utah	.2	0
New Jersey	.2	2.1	Vermont	.5	0
New Mexico	6.0	.7	Virginia	3.4	16.2
New York	.3	1.8	Washington	.2	.7
North Carolina ..	2.6	15.8	West Virginia ...	1.6	3.4
North Dakota ...	.6	10.0	Wisconsin	.3	.6
Ohio	.2	1.2	Wyoming	.4	0

The taxpayers' dollar for public education in the South is divided between schools for white children and schools for Negro children. The average expense per white pupil in nine southern states in 1939-40 was 212 per cent greater than the average expense per Negro pupil. Specifically, the taxpayer paid $18.82 to educate his Negro citizens and $58.69 to educate his white citizens. In Mississippi the expense per white pupil was 606.6 per cent more than the expense per Negro pupil. North Carolina, on the other hand, has gone far toward eliminating discrimination in the distribution of funds. Expense per white pupil in North Carolina was only 62.6 per cent greater than expense per Negro pupil.

The decade between 1930 and 1940 has shown considerable progress. During this period the average expenditure per Negro pupil in the South has increased by 22 per cent. Still, there is a long road ahead before the education of the Negro and the white is equalized. In 1939-40, 82 per cent of all Negro elementary schools and 50 per cent of the Negro high schools in eight southern states and the District of Columbia were one- and two-teacher schools. Many of these were mere shanties. Negro children received on the average 156 days of education per school term in the South in 1941-42, while white children received 171. In many communities the children went to school for five or six months during the year. On the credit side we find that the percentage of Negroes between the ages of five and twenty-one attending schools increased in the decade between 1930 and 1940 from 49.3 to 53.1. But absences were still 1.2 times as high for Negroes as they were for whites.

Racial inequalities in the fields of higher and professional education are even greater than those in primary and secondary education. In 1939-40 there were in the United States—

One white student in college for every 81 white persons in the population.

One Negro student in college for every 225 Negro persons in the population.

Enrolled in institutions supported at public expense are 53.9 per cent of the white college students in the South. Only 8.9 per cent of the Negro college students are in tax-supported colleges. Although at least one undergraduate college for Negroes is located in each southern state, the course of study available to Negroes is greatly limited. Less than 5 per cent of the Negro colleges in the South are on the approved list of the Association of American Colleges—a "must" before credit for work at one college will be given at another recognized institution. In not one of the southern states is there a Negro institution which offers work leading to the doctorate, although there are thirteen such schools for whites. There are only two schools of medicine for Negroes in the South as compared with thirty-one for whites, and three schools of law for Negroes compared with thirty-three for whites. Only one school of engineering exists in the South for Negroes, compared with thirty-four for whites. Moreover, there are no public colleges at all in the South where

Negroes can specialize in medicine, dentistry, engineering, social service, or pharmacy.

The United States Office of Education reported in 1942: "No state makes adequate provisions, when measured in terms of its provision for white persons, for the graduate education of Negroes."

A comparison of the average public school expenditures for Negro and white children shows a substantial disparity between the two. The 1943-44 figures present this picture:

Average public school expenditure per child per year for the
    country as a whole $116.99
Average public school expenditure per child per year in the
    31 states having nonsegregated school systems 131.36
Average public school expenditures for each white child in
    the states which have segregated systems 84.79
Average for each Negro child in the states which have segre-
    gated systems 36.97

Here is the average public school expenditure per child per year in ten states with segregated systems:

STATE	WHITE	NEGRO
Alabama	$ 70.20	$25.65
Arkansas	61.03	25.81
Florida	95.96	47.44
Georgia	73.79	23.63
Louisiana	121.32	40.25
Maryland	115.52	90.82
Mississippi	71.65	11.96
North Carolina	71.60	50.07
South Carolina	82.43	26.85
Texas	92.69	63.12

Teachers' salaries for Negroes were far below those received by white teachers. The average salaries of elementary and secondary school teachers in 1939-40 were distributed as follows:

STATE	WHITE	NEGRO
Average	$1,046	$ 601
Alabama	878	412
Arkansas	636	375
Delaware	1,715	1,500
Florida	1,148	585
Georgia	924	404
Kentucky	853	522
Louisiana	1,197	509
Maryland	1,689	1,446
Mississippi	776	232
Missouri	1,153	1,258
North Carolina	1,027	737
Oklahoma	1,016	993
South Carolina	953	371
Tennessee	909	580
Texas	1,138	705
Virginia	987	605
West Virginia	1,189	885

Negro teachers almost invariably are paid less than white teachers, although the United States Supreme Court decision, making it necessary to pay equal salaries for equal preparation, has been a constructive force in reducing inequalities. Various states, such as Virginia and North Carolina, have taken steps to equalize the salaries of both white and Negro teachers. However, in other states this has not yet been done.

Less money is appropriated for the education of the Negro child throughout the South than for that of the white pupil. For example, during 1945-47 Texas appropriated $27,711,645 for white institutions and $851,804 for Negro schools. Moreover, the total value of public school property for whites was $290,471,798; for Negroes it was $17,261,050. Despite the fact that white schools received twenty-seven times as much as the colored, the pupil enrollment for whites was five times that of Negroes—1,087,264 white pupils compared with 216,059 Negroes. There were ten times as many white high school graduates as Negro, and thirty times as many white students in higher educational institutions as there were Negroes. Out of Mississippi's 100 high schools for Negroes none is accredited. The teachers' average salary in 1939-40 was $4.46 a week. It has been increased slightly since then, but not enough to make much difference.

For more than a decade the National Association for the Advancement of Colored People has brought suits into court to test the premise that Negro and white teachers should receive equal salaries. In most instances the courts have held that under the Constitution both the Negro and white teachers must receive equal pay. But some states have devised means of getting around this court decision. They agree to give teachers equal pay, but they insist that the teachers must be graduates of accredited colleges to receive the higher salaries.

In a study conducted by the *Pittsburgh Courier,* the case of teachers in Jefferson County, Alabama, is cited. Here, after the federal court ruled that all teachers, regardless of color, must receive equal pay, the county school board announced a new plan for raising salaries. Graduates of accredited colleges, rated by the Southern Association of Colleges and Secondary Schools, would be in the A category, those not qualified would be in the B class. Actually, most of the county's Negro teachers were trained at the State Teachers College and Alabama Agricultural and Mechanical College, neither of which is on the approved list. All four of the teachers' colleges attended by white teachers are on the approved list.

Why do the Negro teachers remain on the job? For the same reason, evidently, that so many of the underpaid white teachers remain. They feel a moral obligation to be of service to youth. A good illustration of what a Negro teacher faces is the case of Miss Florence Christmas, a schoolteacher at Copiah County, Mississippi. Miss Christmas appeared before the United States Committee on Education and Labor at the 79th Congress.

"I teach in a three-teacher-type school, with an enrollment of

190 children," she told the Senate. "The average daily attendance is around 160. There are two other teachers who work with me. I am the principal and have had almost two years of college work. The primary teacher has had one year of college training and gets a salary of $288 for the term, or $48 per month. The second teacher, with two or more years of college training, gets a salary of $342 for the term, or $57 per month. The principal receives a salary of $360 or $60 per month. My school term is for six months.

"Some of the people in the community are small-truck farmers. They have a great love for education. They built their own schoolhouse. It has grown from one room to a three-teacher-type school. The money for the building was raised by the teachers, children, and patrons. We gave programs, entertainments, secured pledges from the parents and friends, and gave money from our salaries to help with the building. We have been able to put on one coat of paint, inside and out.

"Our project for this year is to raise money to finish paying for the paint, which is $12.57. Of course, the amount was more than that, but we have raised the money to pay the bill down to only $12.57 and our project is to get tables and benches so that all the children may have seats, especially those in the primary room, and to continue our program for the lunchroom. My school term has increased from five to six months in the past six years, and my monthly salary has grown from $28 to $34, $38, $51, and now to $60—from $168 to $360 per year."

Although the county provides a maximum of six months, the teachers themselves have supplemented that by an additional month. The money is raised from the farmers; the teachers work for less salary for the extra month than the salary paid by the county. The money does not come from the state.

"What do you do the rest of the time when you are not teaching?" Senator J. William Fulbright asked.

"The last four years I worked, beginning the last of March until June, at a factory. We make containers for vegetables," Miss Christmas answered.

"You make more money there than you make teaching?" the senator asked.

"I make almost more in one week in the factory than I make in a month teaching," she answered.

"Why do you do teaching?" Senator Fulbright queried.

"Teaching is my profession," Miss Christmas said simply. "I would rather teach."

The annual expense per pupil in average daily attendance for 1939-40 breaks down this way:

STATE	WHITE	NEGRO
Alabama	$47.59	$14.63
Arkansas	36.87	13.73
Florida	69.76	26.95
Georgia	55.56	16.95
Louisiana	77.11	20.59
Mississippi	52.01	7.36
North Carolina	46.02	28.30
South Carolina	57.33	15.42
Texas	72.72	28.49

Negro teachers are not so adequately trained as white teachers. A tabulation of the training of Negro teachers in a selected group of nine counties in Mississippi in 1940 by the State Department of Education showed that the majority had a junior or senior high school education. Some were teaching who had only a third-, fourth-, fifth-, or sixth-grade education. Moreover, the Negro teacher has many problems that the teacher in white schools does not have. As a rule the former cannot get graduate courses in her own community—she may have to travel far distances to receive such training. She does not get paid enough to travel, buy books, attend lectures, or go to concerts. In large measure she is cut off from these cultural advantages.

Pointing to the low standard of public education for Negroes in the southern states, Doxey Wilkerson notes, in a report prepared for the government: "In general, and especially in rural areas, Negro elementary pupils attend extremely impoverished, small, short-term schools, lacking in transportation service, void of practically every kind of instructional equipment, and staffed by relatively unprepared, overloaded teachers whose compensation does not approximate a subsistence wage. The vast majority of pupils progress through only the primary grades of these schools. The few who finish the elementary grades find relatively little opportunity, especially in rural areas, for a complete standard secondary education. Opportunities for education in public undergraduate colleges are even more limited, and opportunities for graduate and professional study at publicly controlled institutions are virtually nonexistent. The disparity between the general status of education for the two racial groups appears to be decreasing only very slowly, if at all."

Many of the Negro classes are held in churches, old stores, tenant houses, or wherever any sort of building can be secured. Comfortable seating facilities and teaching materials are lacking in many systems. Dr. Wilkerson reports: "In hundreds of rural schools there are just four blank, unpainted walls, a few old rickety benches, an old stove propped up on brickbats, and two or three boards nailed together and painted black for a blackboard. In many cases this constitutes the sum total of the furniture and teaching equipment."

While this is not a typical condition—I saw many schools for Negroes that were comparable in every respect to the good schools for white children—yet it exists in far too many instances to be considered unusual. It is little wonder that the young Negro children drop out of school at an early age, discouraged, deprived of the sound educational background which could help them become better American citizens. An example of what this means to the nation is found in a study conducted by an armed forces induction station covering the states of North Carolina, South Carolina, Georgia, Alabama, Mississippi, and Louisiana. This is a summary of the educational status of selectees received at this station during June, July, and August, 1943:

Per cent of selectees who had not completed first grade:

	WHITE	COLORED
June	3.43	18.43
July	4.45	23.52
August	4.13	28.71

Per cent of selectees who had not completed seventh grade:

	WHITE	COLORED
June	32.62	76.72
July	35.99	81.06
August	36.39	83.62

Per cent of selectees who had not completed eleventh grade:

	WHITE	COLORED
June	66.08	96.98
July	67.76	95.98
August	66.51	96.32

Here we see the effects of the neglect of Negro education. There is a distinct and positive correlation between the money allocated by the state for educational purposes and the educational status of the people. Those states that spend large sums on education made better records in the draft and on other counts. It is known that the Negro selectees from the northern states were superior to the Negro selectees in the South.

Fortunately, the situation is not altogether hopeless. Educators are seeking ways to remedy this situation, but it is a slow process. The southern states have started to equalize the salaries between Negro and white teachers. Plans have been made for the construction of new buildings and the preparation of new courses of study to meet the needs of the Negroes. One of the goals of the Louisiana Education Foundation is to improve the status of the Negro schools. Similar organizations have been founded elsewhere, bent on helping to equalize educational opportunities.

On my tour a noted county superintendent in the South showed me the beautiful, modern consolidated rural school for white children in his county. He praised it highly, and well he might; it was indeed the final word in sound educational construction and practice. The teachers were alert, competent, well prepared; the curriculum had been organized around the needs of the children. The school was equipped with splendid supplies and materials. The pupils had hot lunches daily; the school worked closely with the community.

Not far away, though, on the other side of the railroad tracks, the Negro schools were in deplorable condition. Children were crowded into shanties and leaky shacks; books, supplies, equipment of any sort were lacking.

The superintendent didn't boast about the Negro schools. He was not satisfied, but, he explained, the county did not allocate enough money. As I left, he said apologetically:

"I hope that the next time you visit us I can show you a consolidated Negro school of which we can all be proud. Maybe we will have a Negro high school so that these young children can continue with their education when they leave us. I won't be satisfied until we help the Negro as much as we have helped the white children."

That is progress. Typical of what is happening in other communities is the instance of the public schools in Montgomery, Alabama. Here is the record of improvement in teacher and principal preparation over a ten-year period in Negro schools:

	1936-37	1946-47
Less than two years' training	93	18
Two years or more but less than four	91	70
Bachelor's degree	16	132
Master's degree	1	30
Total	201	250

Various districts in the South are seeking means to improve Negro education and in that way to better the community itself. Workshops for Negro teachers, held in Ascension Parish, Louisiana, have helped raise the community standards. The teachers discuss such problems as discipline, poor attendance, poor working conditions, inattention, and emotional upsets. Instructional supplies more in keeping with the needs of the children and the communities are made by the teachers themselves. Here are excerpts taken from the teachers' reports of supervisory follow-up visits, indicating the success of the workshops in reaching the community:

"In one community seven Jersey cows have been purchased. Preschool children and mothers have been attended by the Parish health nurse and doctor. The kitchen has been screened by the patrons, tables have been painted, a walk has been built, a cloakroom improvised. The trees around the school and some homes have been whitewashed. Two homes have been painted. Five homes have been purchased."

In another school, the report says: "The kitchen has been improved with adequate storage space for foods and dishes. A two-compartment sink has been installed. Cloakrooms have been made. Sixteen deep wells have been dug in the community. Three homes have been remodeled; nine homes have installed electricity and three, natural gas. Nine purebred cattle have been purchased—forty-eight hogs have been killed, salted, and sugar-cured."

Many Negro teachers are eager to improve their own status so that they can do a better job in the community. Typical is the case of an elementary schoolteacher in Rutherford County, Tennessee, who makes $886 a year. She observes:

"With the cost of living as high as it is at present, I must scheme constantly to be able to purchase the necessities of life from the funds we have available. We have no money available for recreational purposes outside of our church and community activities. As important as I know travel to be in the education of teachers, I have been out of my state only twice—once to Cincinnati and once to Indianapolis.

"Many of my fellow teachers in the Negro schools of Rutherford County have left their positions in recent years to accept better-paying jobs elsewhere. I have been sorely tempted. Only recently I was offered a position as a maid to an elderly lady which would have paid me considerably more than I am now making teaching school. Almost any position I might get as waitress, cook, factory worker, or beauty parlor assistant would pay me, on an annual basis, more money than I am now making teaching school. I have remained in teaching because I believe it is my calling. I enjoy working with children and feel that I am making a worth-while contribution to my community. Otherwise, I would have left the teaching profession long ago."

Country-wide, the Negro population has attained a much lower educational status than the white adults. This is true on every level, and covers urban, rural-nonfarm and rural-farm districts. This table, showing the median of school years completed (1940) for persons twenty-five years old and over, is significant:

STATE	*Urban*		*Rural-nonfarm*		*Rural-farm*	
	NATIVE WHITE	NEGRO	NATIVE WHITE	NEGRO	NATIVE WHITE	NEGRO
Mississippi	11.7	5.8	9.9	5.0	8.1	4.3
Utah	11.5	8.4	10.1	..	9.4	..
California	11.4	8.5	9.6	7.3	8.8	6.8
Nevada	11.3	7.6	10.5	8.2	9.0	..
South Carolina	11.3	4.8	8.2	3.8	7.7	3.5
Florida	11.0	5.8	8.7	4.3	7.8	3.8
North Dakota	11.0	..	8.8	..	8.1	..
Washington	11.0	8.2	9.4	7.9	8.6	7.6
Arizona	10.9	7.6	9.2	7.3	8.5	6.6
Wyoming	10.9	7.9	10.0	7.5	8.7	..
Idaho	10.8	7.5	9.0	7.0	8.7	7.4
Nebraska	10.8	8.0	8.9	7.5	8.4	..
Oregon	10.8	8.4	9.1	8.0	8.6	..

STATE	Urban		Rural-nonfarm		Rural-farm	
	NATIVE WHITE	NEGRO	NATIVE WHITE	NEGRO	NATIVE WHITE	NEGRO
Massachusetts	10.7	8.2	10.4	6.9	9.8	2.2
Montana	10.7	8.0	9.1	..	8.5	..
South Dakota	10.6	8.6	8.8	..	8.2	..
Texas	10.6	6.8	9.3	5.7	8.0	5.3
Colorado	10.5	8.5	8.9	7.5	8.5	7.7
Arkansas	10.4	6.3	8.3	5.3	7.4	4.6
Oklahoma	10.4	7.6	8.3	6.3	7.7	6.0
Alabama	10.3	5.6	8.2	4.5	7.1	3.7
North Carolina	10.3	5.8	8.2	5.0	7.2	4.4
Vermont	10.3	8.1	9.0	..	8.6	..
Maine	10.2	8.2	9.5	7.6	8.8	..
Georgia	10.0	5.1	8.6	4.0	7.2	3.5
Iowa	10.0	8.0	8.8	7.1	8.4	7.7
Minnesota	10.0	8.4	8.7	7.8	8.1	..
Virginia	10.0	5.9	8.3	4.8	7.3	4.1
New Mexico	9.9	7.4	7.8	7.1	7.2	6.2
Kansas	9.8	8.0	8.8	7.5	8.4	7.7
Michigan	9.8	7.6	8.8	7.0	8.3	7.4
Delaware	9.6	6.6	8.9	5.6	8.0	5.1
Ohio	9.4	7.4	8.6	6.9	8.3	7.2

There is every reason to believe that when the general standards of education improve in the South the standards of Negro education will likewise be raised. Americans do not want educational discrimination in this country. It is contrary to every tenet and tradition of our democratic land. Progress has been made during the past quarter century. If the rate of progress can be maintained, the Negro children of the next generation will have greater opportunities to enjoy the fruits of a democratic land than many have had in the past.

The low state of Negro education is a challenge to the American way of life. A well-educated, intelligent electorate, regardless of race, creed, or color, is the best assurance that America will continue as a democracy.

AMERICAN colleges and universities, jammed beyond capacity, are facing very serious problems. During the war the colleges were in trouble because the student body had dwindled to a mere trickle. Selective service had taken most of the eligible young men from the campuses; in many institutions only a skeleton force of students and faculty members remained.

Now, however, the problems are of a diametrically opposite nature. The colleges and universities are flooded with applicants; many institutions have jumped in enrollment overnight, increasing their student body by 100 per cent or more. So-called "little" colleges have become big; the universities have become giants, going as high as 40,000 to 50,000 students on some campuses.

With this tremendous enrollment have come problems of readjustment. Many of the institutions are facing a financial breakdown; a student's tuition fees do not pay for the cost of his education; the college suffers a substantial loss on every student that it admits. With the onrush of veterans after the war, the colleges found themselves going deeper and deeper into debt. Many turned to the federal government for help in maintaining their institutions. Others conducted fund-raising campaigns to secure revenues. Still others were forced to borrow on their endowment or from the banks in order to continue.

The colleges' plight has been caused by the tremendous influx of students, and more particularly veterans. The college population has grown steadily during the past century. Enrollment increased two and one-half times from 1900 to 1920, going from 237,592 to 597,857, and again two and one-half times from 1920 to 1940, when it went from 597,857 to 1,493,203. Many informed educators estimate that by 1960 the enrollment will reach 3,500,000.

During 1947 one person in each seventy of our population of 140,000,000 was attending college. Fifty-five per cent of the total number of students were veterans. Soon after the war, the veterans flocked to the colleges and universities, eager to make up for lost time. The G.I. bill, which provided free tuition and maintenance grants ranging from $65 to $90 a month, gave many the opportunity they would otherwise not have had.

Faced by an unprecedented boom, the colleges are concerned over their expansion policies. In a sense they are saying: We will admit the students if we have facilities for them. At present the colleges do not have sufficient room. A study compiled by Dr. Ernest V. Hollis of the United States Office of Education shows that 900 American colleges and universities will need a plant expansion of 93 per cent by 1950 to meet anticipated needs. This means in effect that the colleges must double their present plants within a few years. If 3,000,000 students are in our institutions of higher learning by 1950, as appears likely, the colleges will have assumed a load increase of 100 per cent within a decade. This is a tremendous undertaking, and one that is filled with dangers as well as rich possibilities.

The colleges, however, are not able, of their own accord, to meet the needs of the expansion program. They can, they report, increase their existing facilities by 28 per cent. The other space can be furnished only if they receive substantial outside assistance. They are beginning to look increasingly to the federal government for this support. At the same time, the colleges are also looking toward their alumni, friends, and the general public. American colleges and universities are now in the midst of fund-raising campaigns aggregating two billion dollars. Never before have the institutions attempted such widespread campaigns. Virtually every institution, regardless of size, has mapped out ambitious plans for the construction of new buildings and the development of greater facilities.

A study made by W. Emerson Reck of Colgate University on the financial status of America's colleges and universities suggests that buildings and endowments are the major objectives of the campaigns. In 90 per cent of the campaigns, some or all of the money raised will go for buildings. Congress gave the Federal Public Housing Authority $178,000,000 for use in dismantling, removing, and re-erecting living quarters for faculty and student veterans and their families. By the spring of 1947 the housing authority had 14,000 buildings under construction. This is just a beginning. Bills have been introduced in Congress seeking funds running into the hundreds of millions of dollars to help the colleges expand their programs.

Even with this help, the colleges are not certain where this expansion will end. On many campuses all types of buildings are jammed together to make room for the students. Quonset huts, barracks, war factories, unused hospitals, and trailers have been moved to the campuses.

Inflated building costs, likewise, add to college headaches. Many college officials are prepared to expand their facilities. They have allocated substantial sums for the construction of new buildings; but the construction will have to wait until men and materials are available. In the meantime, the pressure on the colleges continues to grow apace. With each passing year the difficulties colleges encounter will increase. We are facing a new era—an era in which higher education for all will become the accepted doctrine. As a result, it is extremely unlikely that the pressures will be removed in the foreseeable future. College expansion will become an increasingly important issue.

Many significant questions come to mind. How large shall the colleges be? At what point is expansion undesirable? Shall the universities be divided into smaller campuses? Will it be more advisable to add new colleges than to expand the existing ones? It is obvious that a point is ultimately reached beyond which the expansion of an institution is undesirable. At the same time, unless the colleges are expanded, or new ones added, millions of American youth will be denied the privilege of a higher education.

Because of the overcrowded conditions, the class size has increased. Eighty-seven per cent of the colleges and universities of this country reported that their classes are larger this year than they were before the war. One institution said that it had to crowd 1,400 students into one lecture room. In other colleges the normal class of twenty or twenty-five has jumped to fifty or sixty.

College presidents decry this increase in class size, and insist that it tends to lower the educational standards on the campus. But there is no way to overcome this upward trend at present. The median enrollment for men in colleges in 1940 was 378; in 1947 it was 622. The median for women has increased from 301 to 384 in this period. Only lack of physical quarters has prevented this enrollment from going still higher in the women's colleges.

Thirty-six per cent of the colleges, or just about one-third, declared that the overcrowding has lowered the effectiveness of their teaching staffs. They point out that it is impossible to overcrowd the classroom and still expect the same quality of education that the students formerly received.

Ninety-nine per cent of the colleges of the United States report that they are in need of additional buildings. The need ranges from a unit costing less than $50,000 to a whole series of buildings at a cost of $40,000,000. In all, the colleges estimate that they will need two billion dollars' worth of buildings within the next ten years. Much of this money has already been set aside, and construction will begin as soon as materials are available.

One of the most serious drawbacks to greater expansion is the inability to secure an adequate supply of competently trained instructors. Thirty-nine per cent of all the colleges in the country report that they are unable to obtain enough qualified faculty members. Many indicate that they have had to lower their standards to get a sufficient number. Other professions are drawing away the best college teachers. Twenty-seven per cent of the colleges report that they have lost their best men to government, industry, and various other professions.

"Not only are government and industry making inroads on our faculty, but other educational institutions which can pay larger salaries are competing, sometimes in ways that do not seem to be too ethical," President Charles E. Diehl of Southwestern University observes.

Columbia University reports that it has lost some of its engineering professors to government and industrial research. This is more particularly acute in the graduate faculties than in the undergraduate school. Roanoke College, Virginia, remarks that thus far it has been able to secure instructors, but anticipates more difficulty in the future, especially in the fields of mathematics, economics, and the sciences.

"While we can obtain a sufficient number of qualified instructors," President James Bryant Conant of Harvard University points out, "we have had great difficulty in certain areas and cannot obtain enough men of the highest quality with considerable experience. The situation should improve, however, in a few years."

Large institutions do not suffer as much as the smaller ones. Because they can afford to pay more, they can poach on the smaller colleges. This parallels to a considerable extent the shift of teachers from the rural and small communities to the large cities and richer school systems.

During the past half century our society has encouraged men to go into law, business, or medicine, but has discouraged their entering teaching. Analysis of careers followed by members of a Princeton University undergraduate organization over a period of fifty years reveals this amazing situation: of the total group of 2,000, representing a fair cross section of Princeton graduates for the fifty-year period, only twelve entered the academic profession! During this time hundreds elected careers in business and law.

"I think all will agree that the most pressing problem for the academic profession is this problem of personnel," Dr. Whitney J. Oates of Princeton observes. "There plainly are not enough good men in the profession. It is not that talent in America does not exist. What it really amounts to is this: Academia's fair share of talent for the last one hundred years has simply been doing something else."

Dr. Oates disclosed the results of an analysis of the graduates of Princeton from 1930 to 1939 who majored in the department of Economics. Twelve men were awarded highest honors and seventy-three were awarded high honors. Of this group of men, only two of the highest honors graduates continued through to the doctor of philosophy degree, and only three of the high-honors graduates. While talent in economics existed, only a small fraction of it entered the academic profession.

What is true at Princeton is true, to an even greater extent, elsewhere. Even with the tenure and security that professors sometimes get, the jobs do not appeal to the most brilliant minds. One important reason is that college professors are notoriously underpaid. Many institutions report that their best instructors leave the classroom because they can earn more money elsewhere. The following table gives the average annual salary of college faculty members:

		YEAR		PER CENT
RANK		1940	1946	INCREASE
Professor		$3,297	$3,983	17
Associate professors		2,737	3,300	17
Assistant professors		2,456	3,006	17
Instructors		1,837	2,355	20
Others		1,750	2,246	20

College faculty members have received wage increases totaling less than 20 per cent, although it is estimated that the average employee in 1946 received a 60 per cent higher salary than he got in 1940. At present the average college professor gets a weekly salary of $65, while the assistant professor gets $58. The instructor must be satisfied with $45.30 weekly.

This table shows the average annual salary paid to faculty members, based on replies from more than 350 colleges and universities:

1940

AMOUNT	PROFESSORS	%	ASSOCIATE PROFESSORS	%	ASSISTANT PROFESSORS	%	INSTRUCTORS	%	OTHERS	%
$2,000-2,999	90	31.9	144	54.8	86	69.9	100	34.3	10	18.5
3,000-3,999	120	42.6	73	27.8	12	9.8	1	.3	1	1.9
4,000-4,999	37	9.6	11	4.2	3	2.4	0		1	1.9
5,000-5,999	13	4.6	2	.7	0	0	0		0	
6,000-6,999	2	.7	2	.7	0		0		0	
7,000-7,999	3	1.1	0		0		0		0	
8,000-8,999	3	1.1	0		0		0		0	
9,000-9,999	0		0		0		0		0	
10,000, over	1	.3	0		0		0		0	
Under $2,000	22	7.8	31	11.8	22	17.9	191	65.4	42	77.7

1946

AMOUNT	PROFESSORS	%	ASSOCIATE PROFESSORS	%	ASSISTANT PROFESSORS	%	INSTRUCTORS	%	OTHERS	%
$2,000-2,999	26	8.6	93	32.9	61	45.2	220	75.1	30	50.8
3,000-3,999	136	45.2	142	50.2	64	47.4	24	8.2	5	8.5
4,000-4,999	87	28.9	33	11.7	7	5.2	0		0	
5,000-5,999	31	10.3	8	2.8	0		0		0	
6,000-6,999	8	2.7	2	.7	0		0		0	
7,000-7,999	3	1.0	0		0		0		0	
8,000-8,999	3	1.0	0		0		0		0	
9,000-9,999	2	.7	0		0		0		0	
10,000, over	1	.3	0		0		0		0	
Under $2,000	4	1.3	5	1.7	3	2.2	49	16.7	24	40.7

What is (or was) the highest salary paid?

	1940		1946	
	NUMBER	PER CENT	NUMBER	PER CENT
Under $2,000	11	3.9	1	.3
$2,000-2,999	58	19.2	18	4.6
3,000-3,999	111	37.0	85	26.2
4,000-4,999	45	15.0	93	28.7
5,000-5,999	30	10.0	46	14.2
6,000-6,999	12	4.0	34	10.5
7,000-7,999	6	2.0	17	3.4
8,000-8,999	8	2.7	10	3.1
9,000-9,999	..	..	5	1.5
10,000-10,999	8	2.7	9	2.8
11,000-11,999	..	..	..	..
12,000 and over	11	3.7	12	3.7

What is (or was) the lowest salary paid?

	1940		1946	
	NUMBER	PER CENT	NUMBER	PER CENT
Under $500	1	.3	..	..
$500-999	18	6.0	3	1.0
1,000-1,499	99	32.8	19	6.1
1,500-1,999	163	54.0	118	38.1
2,000-2,500	17	5.6	142	45.8
Over $2,500	4	1.3	28	9.0

The highest salary received by professors was $12,000, paid in only eleven institutions in the country. The lowest salary paid amounted to less than $1,000. An average professor received $3,297 a year in 1940; an instructor, $1,837. A number of colleges report that there has been no change in the salary range, or at most a 5 to 10 per cent increase.

After twelve years of teaching, the chairman of a psychology and education department in an eastern college received $3,200 a year. Three months ago he left to do personnel work with an airplane company at $6,800. A professor of chemistry for many years in a medium-sized western institution received $3,900; he left to take a $7,200 job in a chemical plant in Chicago.

"Compensation per hour in industry is up over 60 per cent and salaries in industry are being adjusted accordingly," Professor Sumner H. Slichter of Harvard University points out. "In order that professors may share to a modest extent in the rising productivity of the country and in order that colleges and universities may hold their own in competition for talent, salary scales of professors should be advanced 60 per cent or more over the prewar period.

"Thus far the administrations of American colleges and universities have done little to raise salary scales to meet the rising cost of living. Few price series have lagged farther behind the general movement of prices than the salary scales of professors. This is particularly inexcusable because never in the country's history has the community been better able to support educational and scientific research, and never has the demand for the service of colleges and universities been greater."

Professor Slichter recommends these three objectives:

1. A minimum salary of $6,000 a year for full professors for the usual two-semester year.
2. Minima of $5,000 and $3,500 for associate professors and assistant professors, respectively. Eventually the spread between the scale for professors on the one hand and the associate professors and assistant professors on the other should be substantilaly increased.
3. A 50 per cent increase above 1940 in the salary scales for professors, associate professors, and assistant professors. This also should be regarded as temporary. In order to improve the competitive position of colleges and universities, salary scales within the next three years should be raised 75 per cent above 1940.

To meet the increased enrollments it will be necessary to double the faculty body if standards are to be maintained. Since 1890 the number of college students to each faculty member has fluctuated from 9.74 to 13.36, with the average being 11.00. On the basis of the student-faculty ratio of 1940, Dr. C. E. Partch, dean of Rutgers University school of education, estimates that by 1960 the country will need 329,000 full-time faculty members. The full-time staff for 1940 was 131,552. Hence, by 1960 we will need 200,000 more faculty members than we had in 1940.

"An examination of the source of supply gives a very discouraging outlook," Dr. Partch points out. "The approximate number of advanced degrees awarded in the United States during the past fifteen years totals 290,000; master's 250,000, and doctor's 40,000. Many of those who received graduate degrees during the past fifteen years are now members of college or university faculties. Thus if all persons who have earned advanced degrees during the past fifteen years could be induced to accept teaching positions in colleges, there would still be a shortage of 100,000 teachers at the peak load. It is quite evident that many of the persons holding advanced degrees are well established in business, industry, and the professions and that the present salaries offered in the teaching profession will be no inducement for this group to consider a change in occupation."

This would seem to indicate, Dr. Partch concludes, that many colleges will be forced to select teachers with only a bachelor's degree just as the secondary schools during their period of rapid expansion were forced to accept many teachers who had only two years of normal school training.

The colleges and universities ask: Where will the money come from if we are to increase our faculty members to meet competition from industry? Although enrollments are the largest in history, the colleges are running into debt. Because the tuition does not pay the cost of the student's education, the colleges expect to go into greater debt as the student population rises. It is estimated that by 1960 it will require an annual expenditure of two billion dollars for operational expense, plus additional money for the building program. In 1947 the country spent $870,000,000 for higher education. Dr. Lloyd Morey,

University of Illinois comptroller, estimates that $1,374,000,000 annually will be derived from these sources: from students, or the federal government for veterans, $439,000,000; from endowments, or annual gifts, $166,000,000; from gifts, $102,000,000; from the federal government for research, $67,000,000; and from state and local governments, probably with federal aid, $600,000,000.

Sooner or later the American colleges and universities will have to face the issue of federal aid. They receive it now in various forms—through the G.I. tuition fees, the money for veterans' housing, and the Army and Navy training programs. But the next step, it would appear, is that of aid to the colleges and universities.

This aid might be given in two forms: either through scholarship grants to the students or as subsidies to the colleges themselves. Probably a combination of both will be needed. It has been suggested—and the proposal has met with widespread approval among prominent educational leaders—that the federal government establish a system of national scholarships. Half of the high school graduates who should go to college never get there because of financial reasons. Studies made in New York, Pennsylvania, Ohio, Iowa, Minnesota, and elsewhere have shown that for every student who goes to college, another one, equally gifted, does not enter.

The scholarship program would not be a radical departure from existing educational policies. Through the G.I. bill the government has already set the pattern. Actually, the money provided to veterans is scholarship money. I believe that the government should establish a minimum of 500,000 scholarships and fellowships for the youth of America. When our college population reaches 3,000,000, that would mean that the government would be helping one out of every six students to earn a college education. At present it is helping one out of two under the G.I. bill. It would also mean, if properly administered, that this country would place a premium upon ability and worth.

If we adopt the principles already in effect with the veterans, the scholarship holders should be paid $500 for tuition fees and a maintenance of $75 a month. In addition, another $100 might go to the purchase of books, school supplies, and incidentals. This would mean scholarships valued at $1,500 each. The total cost to the government would be $750,000,000 a year; at the end of four years it would amount to $3,000,000,000. While this may appear to be a staggering sum, it is not more than the government is now paying to the veterans in the form of educational benefits. In terms of relative value, it would be somewhat less than our 1947 tobacco bill, and about one-third of our alcohol bill.

In his 1947 Ingalls lecture before the Harvard Graduate School of Education, Dr. Ordway Tead, chairman of the New York City Board of Higher Education, recommended development of national scholarships as the most feasible method of equalizing educational opportunities beyond the high school. "I see no grave obstacle to the working out of an educationally sound and wise selection which will keep scholarship awards on a high plane of national usefulness," Dr. Tead said. "A federally supported and locally administered plan of scholarships and fellowships is one of the most vital planks in a platform to equalize educational opportunity beyond the secondary school."

The other method would be that of direct federal aid to the colleges, either in the form of outlays for capital purposes, grants-in-aid to increase teachers' salaries, or funds for operating expenses. This is a controversial subject; I have attended many conferences of college administrators and officials at which the issue of federal aid to higher education has been raised. Wherever that happened, two schools of thought immediately clashed: one held that federal aid can be attained without federal control, the other insisted that federal aid would inevitably mean federal control and hence the death knell of the private institution. The federal government has shown that federal aid can be granted to colleges—as witness the land-grant colleges—without undue federal control. There is no reason to assume that the federal government would come into the colleges and attempt to run them. It is difficult to see how this country can operate an expanded program of higher education, a program that is essential for the survival of democracy today, unless we broaden the opportunities available for men and women beyond high school age.

That the plight of the colleges cannot be brushed lightly aside appears evident. The total expenses of the average American college and university have increased by more than 50 per cent since Pearl Harbor. The colleges face a serious financial crisis. Salaries have increased, operating expenses are up, fixed costs have skyrocketed, the total returns on investment have dropped, and enrollment has increased. The colleges must seek money from other sources or they will have to close. The logical method of getting more money is to raise the tuition rates. During the past half-dozen years, 80 per cent of the colleges increased their rates as much as 100 per cent. On the average, the tuition rates have gone up 20 per cent in five years. Still further increases are contemplated. However, the point has already been reached where the tuition is too high for the average student. In some instances tuition has jumped from $350 to $500 and then to $650.

Then again, raising tuition will destroy the very purpose of our higher institutions—that of providing an education for all who are worthy and qualified, regardless of their station in life. The colleges themselves point to four possible solutions: they can raise tuition further; they can seek more annual gifts; they can hold financial campaigns; or they can work for federal scholarships. Actually, no one of these methods will be sufficient; the colleges will have to work out a program that will cover all four.

"Tuition rates cannot be increased beyond a level consistent with the income of the majority of American families," President Lincoln B. Hale of Evansville College points out.

Perhaps President J. P. Wernette of the University of New Mexico represents the point of view of the majority of colleges when he remarks:

"The plain truth is that although the emergency may be over for the country, the emergency is just beginning for the colleges and universities. The states or the federal government will have to give greatly increased financial support to the public institutions if they are to do the job properly of educating veterans as a grateful nation wants it to be done. In some form or other the G.I. Bill of Rights should be extended to the institutions as well as to the veterans."

A pessimistic position is taken by President John C. West of the University of North Dakota. Decrying the fact that larger institutions are raiding the educational staffs of the smaller, and small colleges in turn raid the staffs of the high schools, Dr. West comments:

"A day of reckoning is coming, not only to the colleges and the universities, but to the secondary schools and even the elementary schools. Better plans must be formulated than those that now exist if the whole educational structure of the United States does not falter and spread its deteriorating influence far beyond the boundaries of the campus and into the social, economic, and industrial world. Only unprecedented amounts of money, together with the liberal use of the best strains in the country, can stem the tide which threatens to follow the present crisis with a future disaster."

President Charles J. Turck of Macalester College sums up the case for those who recognize that the colleges must receive help. As former president of the Association of American Colleges, he speaks from a fund of vast experience:

"The rising costs of services and materials affect colleges and universities as they affect every other kind of business enterprise. We cannot pass on these costs by continually raising tuition without putting college education beyond the reach of middle-class families. The large fortunes that sustained colleges have been depleted by taxation or divided by inheritance. New donors on the grand scale are hard to locate and to interest. The outlook ahead for the small college is not good, but America would not be America without these colleges. New friends must be found."

During the war, every college appointed postwar curriculum committees. These committees delved into the problem of setting up a program that might function when peace came. Harvard, Yale, Princeton, Columbia, Dartmouth, and all the major colleges have announced their curricular revisions. Many of the smaller colleges, too, are readjusting their programs to meet the needs of the veterans. The colleges have adopted long-range plans to improve higher education in this country.

College presidents, by and large, expect to see increased enrollments during the next ten years. Sixty per cent predict that the enrollments would go higher, 23 per cent said that they would remain about the same, and 17 per cent estimate that enrollments would go lower. Sixty-two per cent of the college heads predicted that the peak enrollment would be reached between 1948-50. Another 26 per cent feel the enrollment would reach its height from 1946-48. The rest estimated that the peak would come sometime after 1950, several choosing a date as late as 1960. The consensus among educators was that the enrollment would level off at about 3,000,000. Acting on that assumption, many are laying long-range plans. Although several sigh for the "good old days," on the whole the college presidents are convinced that the new era ahead will be one of scholarship rather than extracurricular emphasis. They recognize that the goldfish-swallowing, rah-rah spirit has gone, to be replaced by one that is more serious, more alert, more in tune with the issues that the world faces today.

To a large extent the new attitude has been caused by the veterans. During 1947 more than 1,000,000 veterans of World War II were attending college. This number will double by 1948, and may go still higher before 1950, when it is expected to have reached its height. Nearly 20,000,000 veterans are eligible for the G.I. benefits; probably 25 per cent, or 5,000,000 will enter college or take on-the-job training. Between three to four million veterans may eventually go to school or college.

Overwhelmingly, the college heads report that veterans are doing as well or better than civilian students. Fifty-six per cent of the colleges say that the veterans are doing better work, 43 per cent indicate it is about the same, and only 1 per cent report that the work is poorer. Columbia University gives a typical comment on the adjustment of the veterans to the campus:

"When the G.I. Bill was first proposed we were afraid that we would face the problem of handling large groups of students with poor preparation, relatively low ability, and only a casual interest in education. Uncle Sam was to pay the bill and we envisioned a rather discouraging quality of student body. Actually our facilities, although extended fully up to the Mother Hubbard stage, are limited, and, from the host of applicants, we have been forced to select the best-qualified fifth—or thereabouts.

"Our efforts have paid dividends. Academically the records of the veterans to date have been outstanding, almost invariably surpassing those of nonveterans. Their seriousness and fixity of purpose have won universal acclaim. Contrary to expectations, few are giving up prior to the completion of their educational objectives. Particularly where sound selective measures have been utilized, the academic achievement has been most gratifying."

A unique experiment, designed to help veterans obtain a college education although they do not possess the traditional academic requirements, has proved successful at Brown University. Although Brown doubled its undergraduate student body, going from 1,400 to 2,800, many other veterans clamored for entrance. However, a large percentage could not meet the standards established by the university. They lacked the necessary subjects, or they had poor high school records. Though they seemed a risk from an academic standpoint, they wanted to continue their education—and they had G.I. money with which to do it. To take care of this group, Brown organized a Veterans College, open to service men and women, and administered by the university officials. The faculty was drawn from the regular staff of professors.

The principle behind this step was, in an educational sense, revolutionary. Brown agreed to admit students who did not have all the accepted college requirements. A number had barely scraped through high school. Others had taken commercial or even vocational courses, and thus were deficient in the fifteen Carnegie units. Although Brown University did not want to lower its own standards of admission, it felt nonetheless that it had an obligation to the returned veterans who desired to continue with their education. Because of the large number of applications the marginal or submarginal candidates had only a wisp of a chance to gain admittance. Yet in most instances they were sincere, ambitious, and willing to work. All they asked was an opportunity to show their worth.

This chance Brown provided through its Veterans College. Veterans who sincerely want to go to college, but find their admission blocked, are considered for admittance. The sole stipulation is that the veteran must come from the immediate vicinity or be within commuting distance. Campus housing is not provided. The traditional admission requirements are waived. All the university asks is: Are you serious in wanting to go to college? Do you think you can succeed? The results thus far have astonished the officials. The veterans, lacking the accepted educational background, deficient in generally conceded "must" subjects such as science, mathematics, or a foreign language, are making remarkable progress.

Explaining the origin of the Veterans College, Dr. Samuel T. Arnold, dean of Brown University, points out that it was started with considerable misgivings and solely as a duty. The first "shock" came when the entering students were given a battery of tests, similar to those given to the regular student body. On the three tests—the American Council on Education Psychological Examination, the Iowa English test, and Co-operative Mathematics examination—50 per cent of the Veterans College students proved as good as the upper 70 to 75 per cent of the Brown freshmen. There was considerable overlapping of the middle halves.

The Veterans College is operated during the afternoon and evening. From 1 to 6 P.M. the students attend classes; in the evenings the laboratories are put to use. Thus the university plant is used all through the day. One important restriction is enforced: the veterans are not permitted to engage in extracurricular activities nor in intercollegiate athletics of any kind. The officials believe that during the trial period the student should devote all of his time to his studies. Everything possible is done to help the veterans; they are taught by the same faculty members as the Brown University students. They use the same libraries and laboratories. Although occasionally they are thrown together with the regular students, for the most part they have their own classes. Possibly because the veterans know that they are on trial, or perhaps as a result of their strong motivation, they are doing a surprisingly good academic job. They know that if they can maintain a C-plus average they will be permitted to transfer to the university proper.

Brown University officials agree that the implications of this project are most significant. For, if so-called marginal candidates can become good college students, the entire concept and philosophy behind college admissions may need to be re-examined.

Long-range planning will improve our colleges. But the dangers to higher education have not ended. During the war the public understood the plight of the colleges. They could recognize that the campuses, down to a fraction of their student body, were unable to operate efficiently or effectively. But they cannot understand why the colleges have difficulties now that they are so crowded.

It is difficult to explain to the average person why the colleges lose money every time they increase their student body. The more students who attend, the greater the loss, inasmuch as the student does not pay for his total educational costs. It is a simple matter of arithmetic. A student pays $500 tuition, but the cost to the college for educating him may be $700. For every student the college admits it loses $200. Obviously, if it has doubled its enrollment from 500 to 1,000, as so many have, it has greatly increased its expenses.

Above all, the colleges must guard against watering down their programs. Too many veterans and other students are dissatisfied with what they are getting. Because of low teachers' salaries it is difficult to attract the best men into the teaching field. And because of the large size of the student body the individual student all too frequently suffers.

From the long-range point of view, the colleges and universities hope to develop a strong, integrated, well-knit program that will meet the needs of the day. But from the immediate, short-range position, conditions are deplorably poor. For the next ten years our colleges will not be able to do the job they would like. It is only as the public takes a greater interest in higher education and is willing to support it more than has been the case in the past that conditions can be effectively improved.

Our democracy, as indeed our civilization, will rise or fall as we develop strong, dynamic, sound institutions of higher learning. Beyond that, it is essential that the philosophy of our colleges be consistent with the present societal demands. It is impossible, in an atomic age, to continue the "education for the few" concept that is still prevalent in certain quarters.

"Higher education for all" may be an altogether too idealistic slogan. But higher education for all who can benefit from it is a realistic position. The experience of Brown University with its Veterans College has shown that we cannot be too complacent about our admission policies. We do not know who is qualified to go to college. We have found, though, that motivation and maturity are essential factors. These are intangibles that are difficult to measure.

In the meantime the colleges and universities of this country need the support and encouragement of the American people.

A vast era of expansion, unprecedented in the long 300-year history of higher education, is before us. With understanding and thoughtful attention to the difficult problems that lie ahead, the colleges and universities can weather the transition period and emerge stronger and more powerful than ever before.

15. Effect of War on America's Schools

ALTHOUGH our schools were not destroyed during the war by enemy bombs, they were seriously damaged by American indifference. The effects of the war will be felt for generations to come. Millions of children yet unborn will be cheated and deprived of a decent education because of our shortsightedness.

The war damaged our teaching staff; it depleted the ranks of our best teachers. Men and women left the classroom and were replaced by those less competent. It permitted the school plants to deteriorate; it cut supplies and equipment necessary for educational progress.

As a result, the nation's public school buildings are in an appalling condition. An immediate postwar building program, costing in the neighborhood of five billion dollars, is necessary. Old and dilapidated, many of them constructed before the Civil War, the buildings are an eyesore and act as a damper on teachers and pupils alike. Statements from the forty-eight commissioners of education show that the school buildings are in need of immediate attention. Only five of the states report that their school buildings are in good condition. Every state in the Union reports that more buildings are needed.

New York and California need $300,000,000 each to provide adequate school buildings. Illinois needs $250,000,000 for buildings, Pennsylvania $200,000,000, and Maryland $150,000,000. Nine states—Alabama, Florida, Louisiana, Minnesota, New

Jersey, North Carolina, Oklahoma, Virginia, and Washington—
will require $100,000,000 or more each for buildings.

Building programs have bogged down almost completely.
Cities that had expected to start school construction as soon
as the war ended are still groping for a way out of their difficulties. The excessive cost of labor and materials has made it
impossible to build. Schools that in normal times would cost
$100,000 will now cost three or four times that amount. Eleven
states listed the construction of their school buildings as the
greatest need at this time for the improvement of education.
They pointed to the unsanitary and dangerous condition of the
existing structures as evidence of this need.

In addition to buildings, the school systems of the country
lack an adequate supply of textbooks, teaching equipment, and
classroom material. Equipment of all kinds is hard to get. In
one school in a large city, for example, a kindergarten class
was held up for a full year because the school lacked four tables
and ten chairs. Twenty children were unable to attend kindergarten for a year as a result of the shortage. This is not an unusual condition. I have seen similar incidents throughout the
country.

Schools have not increased their budgets to any great extent
in a decade. At present, it is estimated, 100,000,000 textbooks
are being used in the elementary and secondary schools. The
schools spend 1.3 per cent of their budgets for textbooks. This
amount will have to be doubled before the schools can get
enough books.

Many of the textbooks used in the schools are old and outmoded; some bear a 1915 copyright. One used in a mid-western
city was published in 1889. I have seen geography and history
books that had nothing to say about World War I, let alone
World War II. Many books, written in the early twenties, are
still in use. In some schools the teachers supplement their
outmoded books with current charts, maps, magazines, and
newspapers. But by and large textbooks are still the mainstay
of teaching.

"Schools often persist in using textbooks beyond their period of usefulness," Lloyd King, executive secretary, American Textbooks Publishers Institute, points out. "They don't have any adequate replacement mechanics; lay school boards see old books in closets and say '*here's books*' even though they may be thirty years old."

Different methods are used for the purchase of books. Twenty-three states buy books and distribute them through state education officials. In other states the school system or the parents themselves buy the books. Total purchases in a normal year amount to about $55,000,000, with the schools themselves spending $30,000,000. Educators are convinced that this amount is insufficient to keep the children supplied with modern books. The cost of textbooks, as of other supplies and school equipment, is on the way up. This will still further restrict the amount and variety of supplies available to the schools.

"I know my teachers can't conduct their classes as they should," a superintendent commented. "But what can I do? We don't have enough books to go around. Our equipment is in bad shape. The building is run down and dilapidated. But we have to get along as best we can."

"How can I teach the way I should?" a teacher asked. "Did you ever try to conduct a civics class with textbooks that are thirty years old? Or run a social science department without any maps, modern history books, or current newspapers? It just can't be done. Yet that is the task that confronts me today. The governor evidently thinks that books are less essential than a new four-lane highway."

The war brought many of the ills of the schools into the open, but many existed long before the war.

For example: In 1923 the city police moved from an old building in New York City. The building was obsolete and undesirable for further police headquarters service. It had only one entrance or exit. The interior was of wood construction and not fireproof. The windows were small and poorly placed, which made the interior gloomy. Nevertheless the board of education took the building on a temporary basis. Yet in 1947, after twenty-four years, the old police headquarters is still being used. Fifteen classes, from kindergarten through the sixth grade, are squeezed into its thirteen rooms. Five hundred children attend.

The useful life of a school building is considered to be fifty years. Two hundred school buildings in New York City are older than that at present. At the present rate of replacement, within a decade one-half of all the city's schools will have passed the half-century mark. Twenty-seven school buildings are nonfireproof or only partially fireproof. Thus, 300,000 school children are housed in buildings which at their worst are firetraps.

What about the building plans for the city? The board of education estimated that it would take $133,899,000 to bring its capital structures up to date and abreast of needs in the first six postwar years. This would provide thirty-four elementary schools, fourteen junior high schools, seventeen vocational and two academic high schools. But inflation has slowed down the construction of new buildings, as prices have risen more than 100 per cent.

The effect of the war on the teaching profession has been severe. Hundreds of experienced teachers are leaving the New York City school system, as elsewhere. Resignations have doubled and then trebled. Seventy per cent of the teachers declare that they resigned or intend to resign because of insufficient salary. In 1946, 36 per cent of those who had passed teaching examinations and had been offered appointments refused to accept them. The refusal rate has since risen to 50 per cent. The number of applicants for teacher-training courses in colleges is at its lowest point in recent years. The following percentages for Queens College of those who declared their intention to become teachers, indicate the effect of the war on the nation's schools:

28 per cent of the class of 1945
23 per cent of the class of 1946
12 per cent of the class of 1947

When students are graduated in 1949, 1950, and 1951, the full effect of the teacher shortage will be driven home. Because of the shortage, New York City has been forced to use "emergency licenses." Although common in other communities, the wealthy city of New York had never before found it necessary to lower its standards to secure teachers. In 1941-42 there was one teacher with an emergency license in the elementary schools; by 1945-46 the number had grown to 871! Even with emergency teachers, the city has found it difficult to secure an adequate supply of men and women for the classrooms.

Typical of others, a Brooklyn schoolteacher describes an average day in the classroom: "The following conditions exist in my first-year class this term: The register of my class is forty, and it is practically impossible for me to give each child the help he needs. There are only thirty-six chairs and tables in the room and therefore four children are obliged to sit at movable chairs unsuitable for these tables; they sit on high stools without back support. What with conferences which I have to attend after 3 o'clock and the number of children in my class, my physician advised me to rest for one complete week in bed, therefore putting quite a strain on the other teachers in the first grade. To date the records will prove that every first-grade teacher in my school was absent due to large registers, taking care of absent teachers' children, plus their own and all the extracurricular work involved."

A similar story is told by another teacher:

"I have thirty-eight children on register and only thirty-three kindergarten chairs. Five children are seated on regular-sized chairs that do not fit the tables they must use. When another teacher in the first year was absent for a week I had twelve other children with no extra chairs for them. We have no supply of blocks, toys, or other material for free activity time which we are required to have. The teachers and children had to supply these materials themselves. It is impossible to give individual attention to so many children, especially when the age range is from five-years-five-months to six-years-seven-months in one class. The teacher is under a terrific strain at all times due to these conditions and many have become ill. We drag ourselves to school when not well because we know no substitute will be called and we hate to burden our colleagues with our class."

Throughout the country teachers have either saved nothing during the past five years or they have gone into debt. Almost all the teachers had to curtail their expenditures for dental and medical care, clothing, cultural and recreational activities. A New York City survey of 3,500 teachers showed that: 50 per cent have reduced or eliminated the purchase of books; 62 per cent have cut their attendance at the theater; 36 per cent have dropped educational courses which they had attended in the evening. Twenty-two per cent reported that they had borrowed money during the past two years, ranging from $100 to $1,000, with an average of $250.

A father of four children, receiving $2,460 a year, observed: "I must teach ten hours or more a week in the evenings and also carry a full summer program. Yet I go behind my salary $80 a month. We have no luxuries such as a car, nor do we go to the theater or opera. I haven't had a vacation in ten years. A month ago I finally dropped my last $5,000 worth of insurance. I have bought three suits in thirteen years. My children are dressed by friends or have been in past years. My wife cannot work as the family is too young."

A study made by three prominent educators, headed by Professor John K. Norton of Columbia University, on conditions in Norwalk, Connecticut, showed that the teachers are unable to live on their present salaries. Appointed by the city officials following the Norwalk strike, the committee proposed a much higher salary schedule than is now in effect anywhere. One hundred and nine of the 133 teachers reported that they had spent more for their living expenses than they received in salary. The average deficit was $807.

Although the war has shattered the complacent attitude of many American citizens and brought to light appalling school defects, the war alone is not to blame. The problem of poor schools existed long before Pearl Harbor, and is of long standing. The war helped bring the smoldering issues to a head. Teachers have never been paid enough.

In *The Scholemaster,* published in 1570, Roger Ascham, a tutor of Queen Elizabeth, complains that "a good rider is better rewarded than a good scholemaster." "And it is a pittie," he adds, "that commonlie more care is had, yea and that amonges verie wise men, to finde out rather a cunnynge man for their horse, than a cunnynge man for their children. They say nay in words, but they do so in dede. For to the one, they will gladlie give a stipend of 200 Crounes by years, and loth to offer the other 200 shillings.

"God, that sittith in heaven laugheth their choice to skorne, and rewardeth their liberalitie as it should: for he suffereth them to have, tame and well-ordered horses, but wild and unfortunate children: and therefore in the end they finde more pleasure in their horse, than comforte in their children."

This sixteenth-century doctrine sounds pretty much like twentieth-century dogma!

ALTHOUGH the normal schools, teachers' colleges, and schools of education are attempting to provide teachers with a satisfactory preparation, too often they are failing in their jobs. A complete overhauling of the teacher-training institutions of this country is necessary. What Abraham Flexner, renowned educator, did for the strengthening and reorganization of the medical schools must be done today for the teachers' colleges.

In 1910 Dr. Flexner issued his famous report that recommended the setting up of high standards for the medical schools and the revision of then-existing practices in the training of doctors. As a result of his report, American medical education soon became the best in the world. Half of the 160 medical schools eventually closed their doors. The rest, to gain Grade-A rating, had to meet certain standards with respect to teaching, laboratory equipment, endowment, and library facilities.

Many educators are of the opinion that the teachers' colleges and normal schools are in the same condition as the medical schools prior to 1910.

"The teachers' colleges are in poor shape," Dr. Flexner says. "They represent poor standards of scholarship. It is necessary to reorganize the teacher-training institutions the way that the medical profession was reorganized and strengthened more than a quarter of a century ago.

"Let somebody who is fearless and impartial tell the truth about the teachers' colleges. It is necessary to bring them into our present-day frame of thinking. Too many of the teachers are doing little more than a mediocre, slipshod job."

A number of prominent students in the field advocate that the revision of the teacher-training institutions might begin with the closing of half of the existing schools. Responsible circles suggest that fewer teachers' colleges, administered more efficiently and receiving better support, would improve the training of teachers.

In addition to the 200 teachers' colleges, another hundred schools of education exist. For the most part they are connected with liberal arts colleges or with large universities. Some of them are strong and are doing an excellent job in the preparation of teachers; others, particularly those located in smaller institutions, are poor and need a complete revision of program and purpose.

It has been estimated that a total of 1,200 colleges and universities, including professional schools and junior colleges, now offer work that will allow students to qualify for the teaching profession. Many states will permit any person to teach, regardless of his educational background. The problem, then, is twofold: that of raising the professional standards, and that of improving the teachers' colleges and schools of education.

Proponents of teachers' colleges look scornfully at the liberal arts graduates; on the other hand, the college men hold that the education received in a liberal arts college is a superior training for the preparation of teachers. The issue, however, is not one of teachers' colleges versus liberal arts schools. It is more basic and comes down to this: how can the teachers' college, the liberal arts schools, and all other training institutions preparing men and women to become teachers, be strengthened?

Too often, it has been charged, the teachers' colleges and schools of education prepare their teachers along narrow, specialized lines. About half the courses that student teachers take are professional and deal with techniques and teaching methods. The other half are general courses in the liberal arts.

In some institutions for the training of teachers, an undue proportion of the student's time is taken up with courses in "education." As a result students become technical experts in how to teach, but frequently they have a shallow knowledge of the subject matter itself. For example, the student will take many hours in the "philosophy of education," the "psychology of teaching," or the "pattern behavior of children" but little else in the fundamentals of a liberal education. Too often, educators charge, the teacher knows a lot about theories of teaching but little about his own subjects. The teacher may know how to teach history, but he does not know enough history to teach the subject adequately. Or he may know the theoretical value of teaching civics, but not have grasped the subject itself.

A challenging attack on the overtechnical aspects of the teachers' colleges has been made by the Louisiana Education Foundation. This foundation, with headquarters in New Orleans, has been set up to help raise the standards of education in the South. It is convinced that teachers' colleges should devote more of their time to the field of general education. Some of the charges brought out by the foundation are summarized below:

Much time—in some teachers' colleges as many as forty-one semester hours, one-third of the entire undergraduate work—which could be spent in achieving a sound general education is given over to courses of doubtful value in education. In one Louisiana teachers' college a prospective elementary schoolteacher is given only twelve hours of English and six hours of mathematics, as compared with forty-one hours of education.

Many of the technical courses which the teachers' colleges feel must be included in their curricula could be made a part of the in-service training of the probationary teacher under the supervision of the officials of the public school system. They could be taught under the actual conditions of the classroom, by schoolmen who have tested their theories and practices.

Until he has reached his junior or senior year the average

college student is undecided about his ultimate career. Yet at many universities it is difficult, if not impossible, for a student to become a qualified teacher unless he registers in the teachers' college at the beginning of his sophomore year. As a result, many excellent prospective teachers are lost.

Another serious problem has arisen. Eighty-five per cent of all teachers are women. Obviously, the teachers' colleges are prepared to handle women, since they are in the majority. However, the necessity of spending four years in what in a sense amounts to a woman's college is distasteful to many men. They want to go to college where they can engage in sports and participate in extracurricular activities.

Teachers' colleges have been under heavy attack from responsible quarters. The Harvard report entitled *General Education in a Free Society* condemns the undue influence of "professional" education, when it says:

"With this struggle against direct political control must come a similar struggle against excessive technical requirements for the teaching license. No doubt some such requirements are beneficial—say, six or eight hours in practice teaching and educational psychology, instead of the sixteen or eighteen in these and other subjects now commonly asked. Surely the hope of a sound general education is in teachers who are themselves generally educated."

Another important issue is that of state certification of teachers. Frequently the teachers' colleges determine the nature of these regulations. In some states the training institutions establish rigid requirements that effectively bar from the profession any person who has not gone to a teachers' college. A graduate from a liberal arts college does not have an opportunity to teach unless he has taken courses in the school of education.

Forty-seven of the states have their own regulations concerning the certification of teachers. In addition, a number of the larger cities have their own system for issuing local certificates. The principle behind the certification of teachers is excellent, but a survey of the certification requirements, conducted by the

Louisiana Education Foundation, shows that tremendous differences exist between states. In many instances the laws actually bar good teachers from a state. For example, Arkansas requires that candidates for certification show a paid poll-tax receipt before their request for a license can be considered. Of course, no one who does not live in the state can have that receipt. Perhaps that is one reason why Arkansas today has 1,000 teacher vacancies and 22 per cent of her teachers on emergency licenses.

Some states, while not barring outside teachers, give preference to their own residents. Delaware, in favoring native candidates, makes this provision: "No applicant who is not a resident of Delaware will be granted a certificate who has a mark of 'D' or lower in the last two years of his college preparation in more than 20 per cent of his courses." It would appear permissible for the state to be taught by its own imcompetents, but not by those from other states!

In Missouri certification is easy for its own residents. The state permits its five teachers' colleges, all the county superintendents, the University of Missouri, and the state superintendent to issue certificates.

Most of the states issue certificates valid for life to persons who have a bachelor's degree plus a certain amount of work in the field of education. Colorado issues licenses for a maximum of from one to five years, Maryland for six years, and Maine for ten. Where life certificates are not issued, renewal of the certificate depends upon successful teaching. As a rule the states do not attempt to evaluate the record of the candidate if his college transcript indicates that he has taken the required number of courses. Accordingly, credit from a small, second-rate institution is just as valid as credit from the leading universities. Under the practice prevalent in most states the teachers' college does the certifying when it passes a student. The state itself does little beyond approving the college's transcript.

In recent years a number of states have passed regulations

that require school administrators to be certified. In the future only teachers who have taken certain courses in educational administration will be able to serve as principal, supervisor, or school superintendent. Stimulus in this direction has come from the committee on standards of the Commission on Secondary Schools, created by the Association of Colleges and Secondary Schools of the Southern States. The association has amended its constitution to read:

"Any person entering a position as principal of a member secondary school, or any position of administrative or supervisory control of instruction in a secondary school accredited by this Association, shall have completed one year of graduate study, the major portion of which is designed to prepare for the principalship; shall have received the master's degree, or other graduate degree, from a college or university belonging to the Southern Association or to some other regional association; shall have a minimum of two years' experience in teaching or administration, and shall show evidence of culture and scholarship in one or more fields."

An examination of the certification laws in this country indicates that too often the emphasis is upon technical and professional courses. The liberal education program of the potential teacher is neglected. It has sometimes been charged that the state certification is designed, in part, to force students to attend teachers' colleges or take courses in schools of education.

Educators generally consider the teachers' colleges to be the "weak sister" of the nation's educational system.

"With only three or four exceptions, no school of education has been adequately equipped," Professor Frederick E. Bolton of the University of Washington, asserts. "Not a single one is as adequately provided with buildings, demonstration and practice schools, libraries, laboratories, research rooms, and museums as are any of the medical schools accredited by the American Medical Association. Modern engineering schools, law schools, schools of forestry, and schools of pharmacy all have material equipment in buildings, laboratories, libraries, and research facilities that entirely eclipse the equipment of our schools of education."

The head of an important mid-western university told me: "By and large the country over, the teachers' colleges are the weak sisters of the educational profession. The bright students will not enter a teachers' college—at least, I know of none who has in my thirty years' teaching experience. It is very rarely that we can recruit a single instructor from a normal school or teachers' college. The quality of teaching instruction is much lower in a teachers' college than in a liberal arts school."

Statements similar to the above were repeated so often that they deserve the critical analysis of the entire educational profession. For, if the teachers' colleges, where the bulk of our elementary schoolteachers are trained, are weak, how can we expect to get adequately prepared teachers?

The teachers' college officials and administrators are not wholly to blame. For the most part they are doing a commendable job; but the program fails because of insufficient support from the state or the local community. Teachers' college professors get a substantially lower average salary than do instructors in the liberal arts colleges or in the other professional schools. The per capita support for students attending teachers' colleges is much less than for students in liberal arts institutions. Almost always the buildings and laboratory facilities in the teachers' colleges are far inferior to those found in the colleges and universities. The teachers' colleges are the first to feel the pruning knife when a depression sets in, the last to get increased support when boom times arrive.

As a result, only the poorer students apply for admission to teachers' colleges. Dean W. E. Peik of the University of Minnesota's college of education, and chairman of the National Education Association's commission on teacher education and professional standards, estimates that 50 per cent of all students in teachers' colleges come from the lower half of their high school class.

A new policy has been introduced at his institution, Dr. Peik points out. The education school at the University of Minnesota now rejects the lowest 40 per cent of the high school graduating class. In time it may increase its standards to admit only the upper half or even upper 25 per cent. Most teachers' colleges, especially those supported by the state, take any high school graduate, regardless of ability or competence. Results on scholastic tests of culture for the last ten years reveal that the average ability of those going into education at Minnesota has been growing lower each year.

"That is strikingly true throughout the country," Dean Peik observes. "Here is one of our real problems. We are permitting too many mediocre students to enter the teaching profession."

To counteract the declining average that has taken place over the years and to protect itself from the other colleges that have higher requirements, the University of Minnesota raised its own requirements in the education school. During the 1946-47 academic year 15 per cent of the candidates who applied to the education school were rejected. That had never been done before.

"Most of the colleges have to take any high school graduate," Dean Peik brings out. "That is one of the reasons why teaching is in such low repute. In many institutions the professors shunt off their poorer students into teaching. If they can't make the grade as engineers, doctors, or lawyers, they are told to try the school of education."

Advocating a complete revision of the teacher-training program now found in this country, Dean Peik proposes that half of the teachers' colleges in this country be closed immediately.

"We are facing two ideologies, the concept of democracy and that of communism," Dean Peik warns. "In developing our democratic way of life no single factor is so important as education. At present we are giving the American boy and girl an inferior education even as compared with the past. This is the most important problem before the American public. What kind of teachers will train our youth? Our democracy depends upon an answer to this question. We are now putting drillmasters and textbook questioners into the classroom instead of teachers who can inspire youth with the ideals of democracy and the responsibilities of American citizenship."

Teachers' colleges have never had sufficient financial support to do their best work, Dr. Paul V. Sangren, president of Western Michigan College, and former head of the American Association of Teachers Colleges, insists. Most of the teachers' colleges have advanced from two-year to four-year institutions during the last twenty years, but their support has not increased accordingly.

"Teachers' colleges have not had the kind of financial support to provide the equipment, instruction, and leadership to enable them to keep pace with the advancing requirements of teacher preparation," Dr. Sangren observes. "Too often the teachers' colleges have been treated as stepchildren in the educational profession. If anything is left over they get the crumbs. The state universities and land-grant colleges come first. Salaries in teachers' colleges have been consistently lower than those in other institutions of higher learning.

"The cost of training a teacher should not be lower than the cost of training a man to raise hogs on a farm. Yet it is. The per capita allowance for the training of teachers is less than the training of liberal arts students, engineering students, architects, or students of agriculture and forestry."

Within the limits of their support the teachers' colleges have done an excellent job, Dr. Sangren asserts. They have been handicapped because of inadequate support.

"If the teachers' colleges are not doing the job, then nobody is doing it," Dr. Sangren insists. "We not only need more money for teachers but more money for teachers' colleges. If you cannot secure an instructor in a teachers' college who is as well trained in his field as one in the liberal arts is in his, then you are handicapping your potential teaching body."

Comments from heads of teachers' colleges and schools of education throughout the country indicate that these officials are aware of their problems and are eager to improve existing conditions. They urge that drastic changes be made to improve the education that teachers are now getting. They offer many concrete ways to improve the teachers' college program.

A plea for broader teacher-training programs is made by Dr. Edwin A. Lee, dean of the school of education at the University of California at Los Angeles: "Greater breadth is needed for teachers in the field of general education. Trainees should begin contact with actual teaching earlier. Longer and more varied practice-teaching experience is needed. More detailed teaching techniques need to be taught. There is still much tiresome overlapping and duplication of subject matter between various educational courses."

Opposed to the present method of certifying teachers, which permits any person who has taken the minimum college work required in his state for a license to teach, many educators are concerned with the lack of uniformity in teaching standards. Because the requirements vary from a high school education to a master's degree, it is difficult to get a nation-wide certification law. Obviously, since education is not a national but a state concern, it would be impossible for the federal government to step in and establish minimum standards. That would depend, if it were to be done, upon the voluntary action of the various states or local school systems. Today anybody can become a teacher. All you need is a little perseverance and the ability to pick up courses in education. Many would agree with Professor Edgar W. Knight of the University of North Carolina, when he says:

"Real reform is likely to be delayed until we have had an end of adding-machine and clerical-bookkeeping devices both in teacher-education institutions and the state agencies that license teachers."

In a few institutions steps have been taken to improve the teacher-training program. Typical of this forward step is the program adopted at Northwestern University. The new four-year undergraduate teacher-preparation program is divided into sixteen units. Eight of these are concerned with large cultural areas and cut across traditional subject-department lines.

The professional training for the teacher studying at Northwestern University begins in the freshman year and continues throughout his entire college career. Early analysis of the needs of each individual student forms the basis for immediate remedial treatment. Dr. J. M. Hughes, dean of the school of education, reaches this conclusion: "Our experience with the new program leads us to the conviction that a teacher-education program planned in terms of segmented courses with student electives, in which perspective is given through orientation courses, is less effective than a program planned in terms of areas with students' choices limited mainly by the selection of teaching fields, but with individual needs of students recognized within the units."

Although students in teachers' colleges are generally lower in ability than those in four-year colleges and universities, they need not be. If the teachers' colleges were to adopt new policies of admission they could secure and hold superior high school graduates. This is taking place at the University of Minnesota, at Northwestern, and other institutions. New Jersey State Teachers College has shown that a teachers' college can select students who are above the freshmen average. Over the ten-year period from 1935-44, the New Jersey State Teachers College admitted students who made better scores than students admitted to liberal arts colleges.

Definite objectives should be established for the teachers' colleges; the primary purpose of education must be, if we are to continue to function as a democracy, to prepare teachers who can train youth for citizenship. To expect superior teachers from inferior material is to expect the impossible. The time has come when the responsible leaders of the nation must evaluate the teacher-training institutions.

Many teachers' college adherents will object—and they have become violently incensed at criticism—to these conclusions. However, this is not intended in any way to "smear" the teachers' colleges or to pit them against the liberal arts colleges. The major problem is simply this: How can we get better teachers? What training do they need to do the most effective job in our atomic age? What courses should they take? Who should teach them? How shall we support our teachers' colleges?

Answers to these questions will provide us with clues as to what the next steps shall be. All the evidence I have been able to gather indicates that the teachers' colleges, the schools of education, and the normal schools are, in the main, in need of improvement. If we recognize the fact that corrections are needed, perhaps we can go one step further and develop a method to meet the problem. Many will agree that a careful study of what is happening to teachers' colleges, where they are going, and how conditions might be improved, will serve a valuable purpose.

Some form of education bill has been introduced in Congress every year since the end of World War I. Although action has been delayed at each session, the time is approaching rapidly when the federal government will have to help equalize educational opportunities in this country.

Two schools of thought have kept the federal bills from passing. On the one hand are those who maintain that whatever money is appropriated by the federal government should go to public schools exclusively; and on the other, those who claim that federal support should go to private and parochial, as well as public, schools. This issue has kept the friends of federal aid bills from uniting their forces.

Probably the bill that has received most support in recent years is the one introduced by Senator Robert A. Taft of Ohio, designed to provide money for the needy states. Apportionment of federal funds to the states would be based upon an objective procedure specified in the law. The apportionment is made in such a way that it bears a direct relationship to the number of children of school age in each state, and an inverse relationship to the financial ability of the state to educate these children.

A formula has been proposed which would give all states a minimum of $40 per year for each child from five to seventeen years. Under Senator Taft's bill only the poorer states would be assisted, depending on the per capita income of each state. Public schools only would receive this assistance. Thirty-three states, according to the Taft formula, would be eligible for help. These would be the neediest states; the other fifteen would get nothing.

The Taft bill does these things:

1. Authorizes federal funds up to $250,000,000 a year to assist public schools in the neediest states.
2. Apportions these funds on the basis of need determined by the number of children and the wealth of a state.
3. Guarantees that every child in every school district of every state shall have at least a $40-per-year education.
4. Guarantees local control of the public schools.
5. Provides for fair distribution of the federal funds in the education of minority races.

Opposition to various other bills that would permit federal funds to go to private or parochial schools has been sharp. Some of the most powerful school groups, such as the National Education Association, have fought this principle in the past and have indicated that they will continue to fight against allocating public monies to nonpublic schools.

"The issue of the separation of church and state is involved," Dr. Willard E. Givens, executive secretary of the N.E.A., points out. "The public schools are our most important asset. Throughout the life of our democracy the most effective influence in our country has been the free public schools in which Catholics, Protestants, Jews, Negroes, and all others have mingled together. The moment we begin to support any private school under public funds we will draw more children out of the public schools. If we subsidize parochial education we will weaken the public schools and thus destroy the one big unifying force in this country."

Another argument raised against federal aid is that federal control will follow. Opponents to federal aid maintain that if the federal government were to pour millions or eventually billions of dollars into the school systems of the land, the government would insist on taking a part in the policies of those schools. "He who pays the piper calls the tune," they are fond of quoting.

On the other hand, those who favor federal aid insist that federal control need not necessarily follow. They point to the numerous federal-aid-to-education bills adopted during the history of the nation. Money has been extended in the form of land grants, outright money grants, and subventions. Since 1802 the federal government has granted to the states for educational purposes land conservatively estimated to be worth over a billion dollars. Another billion dollars has been granted to the states for school support; this includes such items as land-grant college support, assistance to agricultural experiment stations, vocational education, and vocational rehabilitation. In the last 150 years the federal government has enacted more than 160 laws providing some kind of financial support to various fields of education. It has never, however, approved a comprehensive federal aid bill for the public schools.

Despite the federal funds the states have not lost control over their educational programs. In no state has the federal government interfered with the employment of teachers, with the school curriculum, with the instructional materials or textbooks used, or in any other way.

On the basis of evidence I have been able to gather, I believe that some form of federal aid bill is essential. Not all the states need governmental assistance, to be sure. New York, California, Pennsylvania, Ohio, Connecticut, and some of the richer states are capable of supporting their own school systems. But what about Mississippi, Georgia, Tennessee, Alabama, and Louisiana? It seems entirely unlikely that these states will be able by themselves to reach the national norms. They simply do not have the money nor the wealth behind them; they support a far greater percentage of the nation's school children than do the more favored states. The result, as has already been shown, is that millions of children are being deprived of a decent education, and in some instances, of any kind of education.

On the question of providing educational opportunity for all, Senator Taft says: "The federal government does have a responsibility to see that every child may have the opportunity which lies at the very base of the whole system of our republic."

And Senator Lister Hill of Alabama adds: "The extent to which our nation will be great in the years ahead will depend upon the intelligence and the character we cultivate in our youth."

Support for the federal aid bills has come from many sources. At its 1946 convention the American Legion, pointing to the critical situation in American education caused by the shortage of teachers, said that it is undermining the educational opportunity of millions of children. It constitutes a threat to the "individual competence which is a cornerstone of national defense." The resolution said further.

"We recommend the consideration of legislation before the United States Congress providing for federal participation in school support, and urge that legislation which adequately protects the schools from federal domination and secures the continued existence of local control of schools receive the support of the American Legion."

In urging Congress to provide aid to schools and colleges, President James Bryant Conant of Harvard has insisted that without federal funds the American educational system cannot function as it should in the years ahead. Federal aid to education, he points out, would help the "crying need for improving our schools in many states and the national scandal presented by the present low pay of schoolteachers."

Every state in the Union reports that it could effectively use federal assistance. The state commissioners of education estimate that they would need well above $500,000,000. This money would go to improve their school programs and equalize educational opportunities for all the children. Asked how they would use the money if federal aid were granted, the majority of states placed "raising teachers' salaries" as the most important single need. Nation-wide, the states would use

$320,570,834 for the raising of salaries, or an average of $375 per year for every teacher in the country. Another $24,000,000 would go to students in teachers' colleges, in scholarships designed to attract students to the teaching profession. An additional $54,000,000 would go for the education of minority groups, particularly in the southern states; and $47,000,000 would be allocated for more and better instructional supplies. A total of $27,000,000 would go for the extension of adult-education programs.

Educators throughout the country told me that without federal aid they saw little hope of developing an adequate program. In many parts of the country the school superintendents and board of education members said that without aid from sources outside their own state they could not improve conditions to any great extent. This is particularly true in the seventeen states where a dual system of education exists and money has to be spent for both white and colored school systems.

Three major reasons why federal aid to education is essential are advanced by Professor John K. Norton of Columbia University. These reasons are subscribed to by those who favor government assistance:

1. Denial of educational opportunity and gross inequality of educational opportunity are far too prevalent in the United States.
2. The social ills which result from denying decent schooling to millions, endanger the whole nation.
3. The gross inequalities in educational opportunity which exist today are primarily due to similar inequalities in the financial support of education.

As for the fear of federal control, Dr. Norton comments: "The bugaboo of federal control of education is just that—a bugaboo. A century of experience with federal aid for education has demonstrated the fiscal mechanism whereby federal aid can go to the states without resulting in federal control of education."

The American Youth Commission in its report, *Youth and the Future,* observes:

"Equalization of educational opportunity should be regarded realistically, not as a charity from wealthy cities and states to their poorer brethren, but as a necessary provision for national security. The children born on poor land are as much citizens as those born in richer areas. Their obligations as citizens are the same . . . their education is a national concern. . . ."

Two national commissions—the American Council on Education and the Educational Policies Commission—in a joint pronouncement pointed up the importance of federal assistance. They held that: "The national waste due to the lack of adequate elementary instruction for millions living in some regions of the nation is rivaled by that resulting from failure to develop a substantial part of our most promising human talent in all regions. The waste in human resources due to lack of adequate education, both for millions of the rank and file and for tens of thousands with superior ability, is incalculable. No future pattern of federal-state relations in education which does not more effectively capitalize our human resources both in the rank and file and in the most talented can be called sound."

Because of the shocking disparity in the levels of financial support provided education in the United States, it is essential that these differences be equalized. This can only be done, the experts are agreed, through federal aid. Millions of children now attend schools financed at poverty levels—far too low to permit them to receive decent educational oportunities. According to the best estimates it would take a comparatively small sum to establish adequate minimum financial support for all school districts. This has been estimated as approximately $300,000,000, which would be enough to set up national minimum support of $1,600 for each classroom unit.

Authorities have reached the conclusion that the differences in ability to support educational programs would not be greatly altered even if efficiently administered up-to-date tax systems were adopted in all states. No matter what type of tax program

were introduced, many of the states would still be unable to
support an adequate school system. You cannot eliminate the
basic differences in the amount of wealth possessed by each
state by passing new tax laws.

In this connection the American Youth Commission notes:
"In proportion to their means, the poorest states make the
greatest effort to support schools. Despite great sacrifice, they
are unable to provide good schools for all the children. . . .
The commission believes that financial support must be provided by the federal government if an adequate educational
system is to be developed throughout the country. . . ." Moreover, the Senate Committee on Education and Labor in the
79th Congress, reached this conclusion: "There are very great
differences in educational opportunity both among and within
the states. These differences have been continuous over a long
period of years, and all of the evidence available indicates that
equally great differences will continue indefinitely into the
future until and unless the federal government grants a reasonable amount of aid, at least to those states having the least
financial ability to support public education and other public
services."

Even on comparatively high tax rates many states can provide at best meager educational facilities. Mississippi makes a
31 per cent greater effort to support its public schools than does
New York State, on the basis of resources. Yet, Mississippi provides less than one-tenth as much financial support per classroom as New York. To reach the average of the nation, Mississippi would have to spend three times as much for schools as
it does at present. In a sense that would mean confiscatory tax
rates for the support of the schools—which cannot be reasonably expected of any state or community.

Appearing before the 1947 subcommittee hearings of the
Senate Committee on Labor and Public Welfare, Dr. Ralph
B. Jones, Arkansas state commissioner of education, pointed to
the needs of his own state as indicating why federal aid is

essential. Of the 446,000 children between the ages of six and seventeen, only 322,000 were in school during the year 1945-46; 118,000 were either not in school or attended so irregularly as to gain very little benefit. Twenty-six per cent of the youth of Arkansas were not receiving an education!

Of those who attend, 50 per cent are housed in poorly constructed, overcrowded classrooms because of lack of funds to provide adequate buildings and employ well-trained teachers. In 1946, Dr. Jones said, 40 per cent of the teachers had less than two years of college and 20 per cent had no college training at all.

In 1946 the estimated income of the people of Arkansas was $1,020,000,000. That year they spent $27,000,000 on public schools, or 2.6 per cent of their income. Appropriations for 1947-48 represent 3 per cent of the income, as compared with 1.5 per cent for the nation. Despite this effort the average salary of teachers in Arkansas is $1,450, or $300 less than the average industrial wage in the state. The teachers are leaving for better jobs. Dr. Jones is of the opinion that only through federal aid will the problem be solved. He cites these two reasons:

1. The children of Arkansas, and millions of others like them, are citizens of the United States and as such are entitled to free, universal, and comprehensive educational opportunities.
2. The people of Arkansas have provided a higher percentage of their income for the education of their children than many other states have provided, and still there is not enough money to do the job as it ought to be done.

Although federal aid for education has strong friends, various arguments have been advanced against it. These are the principal ones:

1. Federal aid would mean federal control.
2. Federal aid should go to private and sectarian schools as well as to public schools.

3. Federal aid would cause regimentation and destroy local initiative.
4. Federal aid is unnecessary as the states are financially solvent.
5. Federal aid would upset our democratic way of life by centralizing control over education.
6. The wealthier states should not be called upon to support the poorer states.

These issues are important, and have stood in the way of federal legislation for many years. Sometimes they are raised honestly, at other times merely as a smoke screen. But there are two sides to the federal aid question. Many persons who are genuinely distressed at the plight of the schools are at the same time greatly disturbed at the growing reliance of the states upon Washington. If every agency turns to the federal government every time a problem arises, what becomes of state initiative? they ask.

Despite these arguments, however, it is the consensus of most educators that federal aid is essential for this country. It can be shown statistically that many of the states cannot provide a basic minimum educational program for their children. Even as the states equalize the educational opportunities within their own borders, helping the poorer communities and school systems, so should the federal government help equalize the educational opportunities among states on a nation-wide basis.

To argue that the federal government should not participate in education is to argue in a vacuum. Federal participation has been taking place on an increasingly greater scale during the last quarter of a century. A series of acts brought the federal government directly into the schools. Relief funds, made available by the Works Progress Administration in 1933, kept many schools open. The federal government outlined in detail how the money was to be used. Relief funds went to establish such educational services as nursery schools, kindergartens, and play centers. The Public Works Administration handled large sums for the construction of new school buildings. Thousands of school-age boys and girls were helped by the National Youth Administration.

This trend has continued to the present day. The Lanham Act permits the federal government to distribute millions of dollars to pay teachers' salaries and erect school buildings in communities where war industries or training centers were established. The national government, by-passing the local and state educational agencies, goes directly into the community and exercises considerable control over the schools. A number of educational projects, amounting to billions of dollars, were undertaken during the war to retrain men and women from peace to war. The federal government provides free milk and lunches to the school children, once again by-passing existing school commissions.

This experience can be interpreted in two ways. Those who are opposed to federal aid cite it as evidence that any time the federal government steps into the picture it means some form of control. But those who favor federal aid claim that a federal-aid-to-education bill, setting up provisions against interference, would take the government out of education. They stress that the federal government will be forced, either now or if another depression comes, to help the schools. Unless legislative safeguards are taken now, there is a danger that laws passed in an emergency may violate the no-control ideal.

As long as we continue to deprive vast portions of our population of federal support we shall continue to have an unsound, inadequate school program. We can talk about raising teachers' salaries; we can emphasize the importance of spending more money for education; we can rally to the defense of the teachers who are striving to solve their problems without going on the picket lines; but the fact remains that without federal assistance a solution of the crisis in education appears remote.

ALMOST without exception, every segment of American society is in favor of better educational opportunities for the youth of the nation. Such groups as the Chamber of Commerce, the National Association of Manufacturers, the American Legion, the American Federation of Labor, the Congress of Industrial Organizations, the American Council on Education, the National Education Association, and kindred influential bodies have gone on record, on repeated occasions, in favor of better schools and colleges.

The National Association of Manufacturers passed a resolution at its 1946 Congress which said in part: "The Congress of American Industry urges manufacturers everywhere to examine in their respective communities the need for improving teaching standards and supporting within the limit of community capabilities the establishment of compensation for the teaching profession that will insure the attraction of competent men and women to the profession and this just and equitable compensation to those already devoting their lives to this important profession."

The Committee on Education of the United States Chamber of Commerce has worked to secure better educational opportunities for the children of the country. Its *Education—an Investment in People* has had considerable influence on the thinking of the American public. The Chamber is engaged in a campaign to secure community action to meet the needs of the schools. The Chamber of Commerce suggests that:

"Each of the more than seven hundred committees on education should be aware of the conditions and needs of their local schools to stimulate a closer relationship between their teaching staff and the community. Strong leadership is urged in collecting and publicizing the facts about both the value of schools and the wisdom of adequately supporting them. Only through full and widespread understanding of the long-range importance and the immediate needs of our schools can America's economic and social welfare be maintained or improved.

"In those chambers presently having no program on education it is urged that immediate steps be taken to apprise themselves of the conditions and relative adequacy of their schools, in order that they may help to bring about a prompt and lasting solution to their communities' educational problems."

The Chamber points out that a close relation exists between the level of education and the economic well-being of the people. In a study entitled *Education Steps Up Living Standards,* prepared for the Chamber of Commerce, a direct relationship is shown between the level of education and the income in ten foreign countries.

"All nations want to be more prosperous," the Chamber notes. "All want a higher income. Many things can be done to help raise the level of income of a country. Better machinery is most important; more efficient management is vital; more effective labor is necessary; wise use of natural resources is imperative; far more research is needed in many fields. In our modern industrial and technical economy it is necessary that both labor and management understand production and cooperate to increase output. Underlying all these, however, is the level of understanding and technical knowledge of all the people."

The study presents evidence to show why any country that wants to raise its level of income should improve its education and technical training. Five poor countries—Colombia, Mexico, Brazil, Yugoslavia, and Rumania—are compared with five rich ones—Denmark, New Zealand, the United States, Norway, and

Switzerland—to show why some are poor and some are rich. Basically, it is due to the educational development within that country. The comparison between Colombia and Denmark will illustrate this thesis:

Colombia is a country that has almost everything in the way of resources—millions of acres of rich land, enormous quantities of oil, great mineral deposits. It has some of the cheapest power in the world. Certainly, if in any place we should expect a high standard of living, it should be there. But the mass of the people in the country lack technical training. They lack the education necessary to use these resources properly. The net result is an extremely low standard of living.

Denmark, on the other hand, has few natural resources but a high standard of education and technical training. The Chamber indicates that a hundred years ago Denmark was one of the poorest countries in Europe. Much of the land was naturally sandy; there were few minerals; the growing season was short. Today the level of technical knowledge and skill of the typical Danish farmer is among the highest in the world. In the course of a single century this rise in technical efficiency of the workers brought an amazing change in the standard of living. The lack of resources did not prevent the development of a high standard of living where the people had sufficient skill.

A comparison made between Brazil, a country of great resources and little education, and the United States, a nation of high resources and relatively high schooling, shows this picture:

Brazil has very large resources—tens of millions of acres of land, enormous mineral resources, timber and forest resources among the largest in the world. The potential water-power developments are among the most extensive anywhere known. Brazil can grow almost all the products known to man. With these advantages one would think that Brazil would have an unusually high income.

Yet the level of education and technical training in Brazil is

extremely low. The average income is low. There is every reason to believe that if the people were shown how to develop and use their resources, there would be a startling rise in the income of the country.

The United States has much rich land, large mineral resources, cheap sources of power, reasonably adequate supplies of timber, and many other resources. There are many places in the United States, however, where the average income is low. In fact, in some sections of the United States there are living conditions about as low as can be found in almost any part of the world. In these places the level of technical training is also low. Even the most advanced communities in the United States would benefit by an expansion of education and technical training. The low-income sections of the country would show sensational advances in income if their educational facilities were increased.

The Chamber of Commerce report stresses that one thing is common to every country with a high income—education. It observes: "You will find that the people have a high level of education and great technical skill. . . . The evidence is impressive that education is a causal factor as far as income is concerned. In other words, if a country will increase the amount of education and technical training, the income will increase. In the light of all the information available, we are justified in saying that the income will increase far more than the cost of the education. The more the education increases, the higher the income rises. In this sense we are justified in saying that more education will cause an increase in the income of a country."

Patriotic organizations, too, support the "better schools for America" campaign. The Veterans of Foreign Wars, calling upon its 2,000,000 members to work for better schools, observes that "the greatest obstacle to the establishment of educational opportunity is public indifference." The Veterans' society adds: "There appears to be a lack of understanding of what we are educating for, what the schools are trying to accomplish, what

problems they face, and how they can be improved. There is
indifference to the necessity of raising professional standards
for teachers by offering proper compensation and inducements
to attract qualified young teachers."

An educational program adopted by the Veterans of Foreign
Wars includes these objectives:

1. Federal aid to education to assure an adequate foundation program of education in every state providing each state is spending in proportion to its ability to pay.
2. Greater state initiative by legislative acts guaranteeing sufficient
   sums of money for adequate schools in every district.
3. Reorganization of small public school districts into larger administrative units to provide greater educational opportunity in
   rural areas with greater efficiency.
4. Greater efforts to attract personnel of superior quality into the
   teaching profession and to make that career sufficiently attractive to retain their services.

Pointing to the crisis in American education, the American
Federation of Labor adopted a resolution advocating adequate
public schools as the indispensable foundation of a successful
democratic society. It held further that the tragic conditions in
the nation's school systems have resulted largely from inadequate salaries, undemocratic administration in the schools, and
political exploitation in the school system. The American Federation of Labor went on record as "urging all affiliated labor
bodies to assist teachers in securing better salaries and better
working conditions not only for the benefit of the teachers
themselves but also in the interest of providing adequate educational facilities for the nation's children at this critical time
in American history."

A similar resolution, passed by the Congress of Industrial
Organizations, urged greater support for education. In part, it
said: "Our democracy must be based on a people who have
the widest opportunities for education. There are many areas
in this country where educational facilities are absent or

meager and large numbers of American people are denied this important right. Many adults, although desiring to learn to read and write as well as to take vocational training and cultural courses, cannot do so because of the absence of adequate facilities. Therefore, we call upon Congress to enact legislation which has been pending for a long time to provide federal aid to states for expanding and developing full educational facilities so all Americans shall be able to enjoy the full benefits of education. We endorse a national adult educational program and urge the Congress of the United States to appropriate federal funds to promote a national adult educational program in co-operation with the several states and administrative agencies thereof."

Only isolated groups oppose the additional taxes needed to support the schools in an adequate manner. An unusual instance of this type of thinking is found in this advertisement from the *Loudon Times Mirror,* Leesburg, Virginia, which appeared on April 4, 1946:

KEEP LOUDON WEALTHY

Here is the record

Six national banks with deposits of $15,143,791.35.

Over $10,000,000 war bonds purchased during the war.

Liquor bill in 1945 of $355,000,000.

More intangible property than any county in Virginia (except Arlington).

More intangible property than any city in Virginia (except Richmond and Norfolk).

Second lowest tax rate in state on real estate and personal property.

Real estate and personal property valued at $55,000,000 (assuming 35% assessment).

Do not dissipate this wealth to hire teachers. We cannot stand another tax raise of 20¢. (Close some schools if necessary.)

Tell your Supervisor that school children do not vote.

THIS AD IS PAID FOR BY TAXPAYERS.

Most of the thoughtful people throughout the country are opposed to advertisements such as the above. The case of the Louisiana Education Foundation is illustrative of how the community can work together to develop a sound school program.

Not long ago a New Orleans high school graduate, valedictorian of his class, applied for admission to one of the leading eastern engineering colleges. Back came the report that if he attended a good preparatory school for two additional years he could be admitted. When the student's father, one of the influential men of the South, learned that the college accepted high school graduates from other sections of the country without additional study, he became puzzled and disturbed. When he learned that many of the good colleges and universities considered the secondary training received in the South to be inferior he urged that something be done to correct this situation.

Something was done. A group of prominent citizens of Louisiana, representing business, labor, education, and industry, joined together to form the Louisiana Education Foundation. Designed to raise the school standards of the state and to set a pattern that might be followed in other parts of the South, the foundation has taken an active part in working for better school conditions for both white and Negro children. Headed by a former member of the Louisiana State University staff, the foundation has crystallized public opinion for fuller support of the school systems throughout the state. Through education, the organization believes, it can improve the social and economic life of Louisiana. It has taken as its thesis the slogan that "good education for all is the foundation upon which the abundant life is built."

In carrying out its program, the foundation has not looked elsewhere for leadership or guidance. It is supported by civic and philanthropic leaders who are anxious to see the South reach the educational standards found in other parts of the nation. The foundation engages in the following activities:

1. Gathers, edits, and disseminates information concerning education in Louisiana and other parts of the country.
2. Encourages and initiates projects that will foster sound educational practice.
3. Makes studies of education problems and situations in Louisiana.
4. Supplies information to all groups which are interested in the educational advancement of Louisiana.
5. Encourages professional co-operation among educators and educational institutions.

The foundation is predicated on the theory that the only way living standards of the South can be raised is to improve the schools. That means both the white and Negro schools of the state. The foundation is now attempting to establish a model consolidated Negro school in a typical parish, to serve as a pattern. Going beyond New Orleans itself, the foundation has mapped a state-wide program for the coming ten years. It holds that the entire issue of consolidation should be examined to determine what school districts should be eliminated in the interest of better administration. There is danger, it warns, that when a school-building program finally gets under way, shortsighted communities may seek to construct one- or two-room rural schools, thus perpetuating existing conditions.

A nation-wide campaign to improve educational standards is being supported by the National Education Association. However, the educators stress that teachers' organizations alone can do little to secure better conditions; rather, the campaign must be a community-wide activity, sponsored and carried on by citizens' committees representing civic clubs, business and labor groups, women's organizations, farm and religious leaders, as well as board of education and parent-teacher organizations.

Answering the question "What can you do to help solve the teacher shortage?" the N.E.A. gives these suggestions:

1. See that only qualified teachers are employed in your school.
2. Make your teachers a vital part of community life.

3. See that your teachers enjoy a normal social and professional life and are comfortably housed.
4. Surround your teachers with the professional esteem that you give to your family physician or family lawyer.
5. Provide attractive and modern equipment for your children's classrooms.
6. Strengthen state retirement and tenure laws.
7. Provide adequate salaries.

As a part of their daily life, the citizens of the community are urged to:

1. Point out the importance of good teaching as a factor in maintaining our democracy.
2. Interest your children and the children of your friends in teaching as a career.
3. Visit your schools and your teachers. Learn about the jobs they are trying to do and what you can do to help them.
4. Establish friendly contacts with your teachers. Give them the same confidence that you give your family physician.

Because of the vast amount of public interest aroused in the schools, caused in part by *The New York Times* survey of school conditions, a number of states and local communities have increased their educational budgets. More significant than the amounts of salary represented—the increases ranged from $200 to more than $600 per teacher—is the evidence that legislatures and boards of education are beginning to respond to the upsurge of public opinion.

Several examples of recent salary increases for public school teachers, indicating that the public is behind the schools, are here cited:

Idaho: The appropriation for state aid was increased from $3,025,000 to $8,000,000, an increase of 165 per cent. The appropriation is a part of a school-reorganization and school-finance program which establishes a minimum-salary schedule in Idaho for the first time. Minimum salaries will be $1,600 for teachers with four years of preparation, $1,800 with five years.

Indiana: A revision of the state salary schedule in Indiana provides for a minimum of $2,400 for teachers with a bachelor's degree—81.8 per cent higher than the previous salary of $1,320.

Tennessee: The state appropriation for schools has been nearly doubled. The former appropriation of $19,000,000 a year is to be increased by approximately $15,000,000. Salary increases on the state schedule will range from 54 to 77 per cent.

Washington: A minimum salary of $2,400 for qualified teachers has been written into the law, and the state aid per teacher more than doubled.

West Virginia: The new minimum-salary schedule in West Virginia will raise the minimum salary for beginning teachers with bachelor's degrees by one-third, the new salary being $1,800. The top salary guaranteed to teachers with master's degrees is $2,889, an increase of 50 per cent over the current salary of $1,917.

When the responsible leaders of the nation, both in business and in education, are unanimously behind the drive to get better schools, we can be confident that the battle fought by Horace Mann one hundred years ago to establish free public education for all will not have to be fought over again.

VARIOUS suggestions have been made for the improvement of the nation's schools. Increased salaries for teachers and higher certification standards are seen as the most important needs today by school leaders. Reports from the forty-eight state commissioners of education point to the urgency of the postwar educational problem. They indicate that it is essential that action be taken immediately if the public school system is to regain its former place in American society. The most important recommendations, made by the nation's top-ranking school officials, include:

1. Increased salaries for teachers.
2. Higher certification standards.
3. Higher caliber teachers—improvement in training and selection.
4. Increased state supervision and aid.
5. Improvements and additions in school buildings.
6. Reorganization of school administrative districts to increase efficiency.
7. Equality of educational opportunity for all children.
8. Assistance from the federal government.
9. Better school transportation.
10. Better health programs.
11. Smaller classes.
12. Removing politics from the schools.
13. Improved working conditions for teachers.
14. Improvement of curriculum.

Many of the states have their own peculiar problems but basically they fall into a similar pattern. The schools are threatened with a breakdown in every part of the country and are seeking whatever assistance is available. Arizona, for example, suggests as immediate steps the increased facilities for state supervision of schools, an improved method of apportioning state aid to ensure a degree of equalization, and the establishment of state and county school superintendents' offices on a professional rather than a political basis. For its part, Oregon calls for a well-trained and adequately paid corps of teachers, together with a reorganization of the present school district system into larger administrative units. Missouri urges the improvement of teachers' status, salary, tenure, and working conditions.

Illinois suggests this broad, all-inclusive program: "A 100 per cent teacher tenure law. A general increase in the level of teachers' salaries. An effective reorganization of school districts with the idea of increasing educational opportunity for all the children of the state. Extension of vocational and adult educational facilities through an effective junior college organization. Financial methods for the equalization of the educational opportunities for all the children of the state."

From Mississippi comes the proposal that teachers' salaries be substantially increased and that a long-term program be introduced not only to take care of the teachers' needs but also to induce college students to turn to the teaching profession. Additional funds for school buildings and instructional supplies, as well as more funds for the teacher retirement system are proposed. Similarly, beyond seeking competent teachers, Alabama urges better transportation and other facilities for Negro children. Kentucky calls for a well-trained teaching staff and for a salary schedule sufficiently high to attract into the profession young people of high caliber and to conserve the present supply of well-qualified teachers. Maryland asks for larger enrollments in state teachers' colleges to ensure an adequate supply of trained teachers. It would be necessary, the state adds, to pay higher salaries to attract the type of people needed to carry on the challenging and difficult work of educating children for present-day life.

A twelve-point program, designed to help schools, has been adopted by the National Commission on Teachers Education and Professional Standards of the National Education Association. Minimum essentials have been set up to raise teaching to a professional status. Conferences have been held during the past year and are scheduled for the coming years to inform the public of the crisis in education. The twelve goals include:

1. Immediate elimination of emergency licenses, but in no case by the lowering of regular certification standards.
2. Raising of certification requirements for new teachers in every state to a minimum of four years of thorough professional preparation; continued progress in advanced states by the adoption of a minimum requirement of five to six years of professional training.
3. Minimum beginning salaries of $2,400 per year for four-year college graduates professionally prepared to teach.
4. Annual salary increases starting with the second year of service and continuing with additional experience and training to a level of at least $4,000 per year for college-trained teachers with ten years of service, with salaries of $5,000 to $6,000 per year for teachers of long experience and demonstrated efficiency.
5. A maximum class size of twenty-five to thirty pupils, with teachers in high schools and other departmentalized schools dealing with a maximum of 100 pupils per day in four, or at most five, classes per day.
6. Refusal by colleges and universities to admit students of low ability into teacher-preparation curricula.
7. Liberal scholarships to attract the most competent young people into teacher-preparation courses.
8. Increase of two billion dollars in financial support for public schools from local, state, and federal sources.
9. Financial support of teacher-preparation institutions by an amount per student equal at least to the average expenditure per student for other types of general and professional higher education.

10. Effective tenure, retirement, and tax legislation extended to all states and institutions.
11. Co-operative in-service educational programs for teachers, with adequate financial support.
12. The same degree of professional and personal freedom and community respect as that accorded to medicine and other professions.

Dr. John W. Studebaker, United States Commissioner of Education, feels that the quality of teaching is the paramount problem in the development of education as a profession.

"The heart of the present crisis in education is to be found in the bedrock question of the quality of teaching," Dr. Studebaker observes. "Adequate buildings, proper supplies, books and audio-visual materials are all important but they are less significant than an assured expertness of instruction and a fine quality of teacher-pupil relationships which together constitute the fundamental of fundamentals of the kind of education necessary to sustain our free way of life.

"Teaching is both an art and a science. We have today too many amateurs trying to carry on a complicated professional process with our most precious resources—the millions of our children and young people. A high degree of excellence in teaching is necessary in this day of crucial problems which are world-wide in their complications."

How is the child to be stimulated?

"The unlimited potential of the human mind cannot properly be cultivated by novices," Dr. Studebaker holds. "If a child is not being stimulated to the best that is in him in understanding, straight thinking, tolerance, and the other qualities which go to make up a competent citizen, he can never fully recover these priceless assets in later life. Our children are capable of infinite development, but the relatively poor quality of teaching which is all too common throughout the country leaves our children on plateaus of learning far below their potentialities."

How can student-teachers get a better conception of what excellent teaching is?

"I think a series of sound films showing such master teachers as Angelo Patri in action with children would do a great deal to help future teachers and parents alike to understand what is meant by excellent teaching," the education commissioner points out. "In fact, I think that a philanthropist or a foundation wishing to make a fundamental contribution to the future welfare of the country could scarcely make a better use of money than to furnish the funds for such a series of motion pictures and related materials.

"Such vital pictures of artistic teachers in action would dramatize, in an unusually effective way, for prospective teachers the significance of the teacher's role. Subtle relationships which are hard to explain in words could be sensed from the visualized situation."

"What do we need in order to produce the kind of master teacher you describe?" Dr. Studebaker was asked.

"We need to assure our competent teachers that they can have security, an adequate salary, good surroundings, and a real place in the life of the community," he replied. "If more people were aware of the abiding satisfactions that come to a teacher who knows his job, we would have more able young people willing to make teaching a lifetime profession.

"The recent rapid development of the single-salary schedule for teachers in most of our largest cities is a very encouraging sign. By this system the elementary schoolteacher with the same experience and preparation receives the same salary as the teacher at the secondary level. The single-salary schedule was put into effect in Des Moines and Denver simultaneously in 1921. The idea has grown slowly but steadily since then. We need public recognition of the fact that the contribution made by teachers of small children is of fundamental importance as a foundation of all later development."

Below are listed certain recommendations and proposals, based on information that I gathered, and on the opinions expressed by laymen and by leading school and college officials. I consider them to be the minimum essentials necessary to re-

store the public school system of the United States to a position
of leadership.

1. *Greater financial support of the public schools*

At present this country spends less of its national income for
education than either Great Britain or the Soviet Union. According to the best estimates available, the United States should
spend 5 per cent of its income for education. This would mean,
concretely, that we spend approximately seven and one-half
billion dollars per year—the sum to vary according to the income of the nation. With this amount, it would be possible to
revitalize the educational system and make it the strongest and
best in the world. Obsolete, archaic schools could be replaced
with modern, efficient ones. Immediately the country should
double its support of public education. Instead of two and
one-half billion we should spend five billion dollars.

2. *Increase in teachers' salaries*

With greater funds it would be possible to increase teachers'
salaries to the point where the profession would attract the
best students in the nation. The National Education Association is advocating a minimum of $2,400 a year. The American
Federation of Teachers and the Congress of Industrial Organizations teachers' union are seeking a $2,500 minimum. Educa-
tors generally agree that the minimum should not be much below that figure. They point out that $47 or $48 a week is not
too much for qualified teachers. It is not too much when compared with salaries earned by other members of the community, skilled and unskilled. The morale of the entire profession
would be raised immeasurably. And higher salaries for teachers
would result in increased dividends for the entire community.

3. *Higher requirements and standards of the teaching profession*

With increased salaries must go higher standards for the
teaching profession. Too many incompetent teachers are certified for the good of the profession or the public. Educators
agree that a minimum of from five to six years of college training is an absolute essential. At present the certification requirements are extremely elastic, vague, and oftentimes contradic-
tory. I would propose that a minimum of five years of college
training be established immediately as a basic requirement for
public school teaching on both elementary and high school
levels. This training could be divided between general education and professional work. A good division might be three
years of pre-education with the emphasis upon a solid liberal
arts program, and two years of professional training in a teachers' college or school of education.

Not many teachers, obviously, could retain their licenses
under the five-year requirement. In view, however, of the enormous responsibilities of the teacher of today, and in view of the
many added duties the teacher is called upon to perform, the
necessity of permitting only the best-qualified men and women
to teach becomes all the more apparent.

4. *Federal aid to education*

Federal aid, divorced from federal control, is necessary to
improve conditions in many parts of the country. Although
there is some difference of opinion on this question, most of the
education profession is agreed on the principle of federal aid.
The chief point at issue is whether federal funds should go to
private and parochial schools as well as to public schools.

Southern states in particular insist that without federal funds
they cannot possibly meet the school needs of their communities. Many of the poorer states spend more of their per capita
income for schools than do the so-called more favored states.

Moreover, inequalities exist within individual states that could be corrected through federal assistance. Expenditures per child or classroom in a city or prosperous rural district are frequently two or three times higher than in poorer areas, as local tax revenues are the main support of the schools.

We are a nation of nomads. Millions of men and women cross state borders as readily as one visits his neighbor across the street. For that reason, education is no longer solely a state responsibility. On the basis of past history of educational support by the federal government, it appears altogether practical to provide the states with substantial sums of money and at the same time keep out federal interference.

5. Single-salary schedule

Many teacher groups have taken up the demand for a single-salary schedule, in which teachers of equal preparation receive equal money for their work, regardless of what grade they happen to teach. Thus an elementary teacher would receive the same basic salary as the high school instructor.

The argument for the single-salary schedule appears irrefutable. The elementary grades are among the most important in the life of the school child. Poor teachers can ruin a child's educational career in the early years of his life. By placing a premium on high school teachers, it has become impossible to get a sufficient number of adequately trained elementary teachers.

Educators agree that the double standard in the teaching profession should be removed. The greatest single barrier thus far has been the question of money. Strides, however, have been made in various communities. New York State has established the single schedule on a state-wide basis. All teachers, regardless of the grades in which they teach, are to receive comparable salaries. The determining factor will be preparation, not the grade level. New York's example in establishing the single-salary schedule can serve as a pattern for other states

6. *Better working conditions for teachers*

Although theoretically teachers have a five-hour day and a
five-day week, with long vacations and three summer months'
rest, in practice the teacher is one of the hardest working
members of the community. She is called upon to do all kinds
of extracurricular work such as yard duty, patrolling the lunchroom, conferring with parents after school hours, going on
Sunday school hikes with the youngsters, and staying in evenings to correct papers and map out lesson plans.

More teachers added to the schools would, of course, eliminate some of the outside load. Teachers should be permitted
to devote their time exclusively to their professional work and
not be hampered with unimportant details that might better
be entrusted to a clerical assistant. Better working conditions
would also include modern, up-to-date equipment and supplies.
Teachers should be permitted to participate in the school's program and work closely with the administration in setting up
the policies and procedures for the school.

Smaller classes are essential for the welfare of the children.
Not only would they make for better working conditions, but
would permit the teacher to give individual attention to the
children. I have seen classes of fifty, sixty, or seventy pupils,
crowded into rooms not meant for more than thirty-five. This
additional burden on the teacher is usually fatal to the educational program of the children. A teacher with seventy children
cannot be expected to give them that personal attention so
necessary in good teaching.

7. *Tenure and retirement laws*

Adequate tenure and retirement laws should be introduced
in every state of the Union. Poor tenure laws make for dissatisfied teachers and for poor morale. A teacher who does not know
from year to year whether her contract is to be renewed is not

in a position to show any spirit of independence or originality. She is more likely to remain mediocre so as not to attract any attention that might single her out for dismissal. But in that way she will not be an inspiring, forceful leader, either.

The many complaints that have come into the National Education Association offices during the past several years from teachers who have been threatened with dismissal or against whom reprisals have been taken are evidence that tenure is essential to the welfare of the children and the stability of the school system. The correlation between better teachers and the protection of tenure is obvious.

Although every state has some form of retirement law for teachers, in many instances the law is entirely inadequate. Better retirement laws are needed to give the teacher that feeling of scurity and ease of mind so necessary for good teaching Teachers should be protected not only against old age but against illness and arbitrary decisions of their supervisors. Although a number of school systems do offer either full or part payment for teachers who are sick, this is not the prevailing practice. In a majority of instances the teacher must pay for a substitute, which occasionally will equal her own day's salary, or she loses the day's pay completely.

8. *Elimination of community restrictions and meddling*

Teachers very often are not permitted to smoke in public; they must pull the shade down before they can light a cigarette. They must not be seen taking a highball, nor is it in good taste for them to go to a public dance. Many excellent prospective teachers will not enter the profession as long as they have to live abnormal, unnatural lives. They admit that teachers should serve as examples to youth, but they resent the meddlesome attitude of the community in trying to run the most intimate details of their private lives.

The all-too-often-enforced regulations against married women's teaching needs reconsideration in the light of present-day needs. Most educators are convinced that married women make as good teachers as single ones. In view of the acute teacher shortage, it would appear wise to remove completely the ban against married women in the teaching profession. The community should employ the best possible teacher who is available, regardless of her marital status.

9. *Improvement of teacher-training institutions*

The teachers' colleges, normal schools, schools of education, and other institutions for the preparation of teachers should be re-evaluated and thoroughly examined. Too large a percentage of the teachers' colleges are weak and inadequate. It is an indictment that the teachers' colleges today are far from filled when the liberal arts colleges are jammed beyond capacity.

A thorough, impartial, and comprehensive study should be made of the nation's teacher-training institutions in order that they may be strengthened and revitalized. This is a task that should gain the support and co-operation of our leading citizens and educational foundations.

10. *Improvement in school facilities*

It will cost nearly five billion dollars to improve the school buildings of the country and put them in good condition. Although this is a substantial sum, it is not more than is being earmarked for better roads and other public construction. Through a sound building program, designed to give the children in all parts of the country modern, up-to-date buildings, equipment, and supplies, we can expect to reap almost immediate and surely lasting dividends in the way of better school programs.

Not only have the buildings deteriorated and the school plants been permitted to run down, but also the lack of equipment and supplies has lowered the educational standards in many school systems. Archaic textbooks or teaching materials should be replaced.

11. *Improvement in rural schools*

Much needs to be done to improve rural education. Educators feel that one immediate step should be the reorganization of small rural districts into consolidated schools. It is difficult if not impossible to give the child in a one- or two-room school the educational advantages he can get in the larger schools. Consolidation has been advanced considerably because of the teacher shortage. Many small one-room schools, unable to get teachers, have been closed down. At the same time, many of the children in these communities have been denied schooling of any kind. It is important that a specific and constructive program for the education of rural children be adopted as part of the general over-all plan for the improvement of American education.

12. *Introduction of modern teaching methods*

Many significant advances have been made in the field of education. In the past fifty years we have improved teaching methods, and have, through the development of professional skills, made it possible to provide a superior education to the child. These methods have been tried and found to be valuable in private schools and in the better public schools. It is essential that modern teaching methods be introduced everywhere as rapidly as possible. Progress in education is just as important as progress in science.

13. *Greater teacher participation in school programs*

A greater degree of co-operation between the teaching body and the supervisors or boards of education would go far toward raising the morale of the teachers. It would help break down

some of the barriers that now exist and would mean that the
classroom teachers would have a greater share in planning and
executing the school activities. If the schools are to run demo-
cratically, the teacher must take a more active part in the life
of the school program. Only under an autocratic system will
the teachers be relegated to the side lines. Where the school
program is dynamic and alive, the teachers are likewise alert
and eager to participate in the development of the curriculum.

14. *A better recruitment program*

At present little is done to encourage superior students to
enter the teaching profession. It is necessary to initiate a recruitment program that will induce promising young men and
women to become teachers. Most teachers' colleges do not have
an active recruitment program; liberal arts colleges do little to
induce their best graduates to become teachers. On the contrary, they are frequently discouraged from entering the teaching profession and are channeled into other professions.

Many of the 350,000 teachers who have quit the profession
since Pearl Harbor were among the best in the country. They
should be encouraged to return to the classroom. By getting
new teachers and inducing experienced ones to return the
public schools may be able to replenish their ranks.

15. *Greater public interest in nation's schools*

Unless the public understands and appreciates the importance of the schools in a democracy, little permanent improvement will result. Evidence that the public is aware of the plight
of the schools exists in many sections of the country. Laws have
been passed to help improve the school systems. Many states
and local communities will pass similar bills during the coming
year. But beyond that, it is important that the public maintain
a constant interest in the schools. Raising salaries is not enough;
the public must understand what the schools are doing, how

they operate, what their place is in the community. Adequate public support almost invariably follows public understanding of the role the schools play in maintaining and preserving the democratic way of life. A sound public-relations program is needed to bring the schools of the country before the American citizens.

16. *Equalizing opportunities of Negro students*

In many parts of the country the educational standards for Negroes are below those maintained for white students. This is not a wholesome condition, and one that a democracy should make every effort to correct. It is important that educational opportunities be equalized for all, regardless of race, creed, or color. The task of equalizing education is not an easy one. It is a hopeful sign that so many southern communities are voluntarily raising the standards of the Negro school children. This is the democratic way.

17. *Better health programs*

Not many school systems have adequate health programs. Doctors, school nurses, and health instructors are lacking. Eyes go unexamined for months if not years; dental cavities remain unfilled; children develop rickets and other diseases that might be avoided with proper care and attention.

One of the major tasks in the field of education is that of building a sound health program for American youth. Often the educators recognize the importance of taking care of the child's mind, but they neglect the child's body. It is only when a war comes to startle us that we are shaken from our lethargy. Thereupon we relapse into our traditionally complacent attitude. The youth of this country deserve a modern health program.

18. *Expansion of higher education facilities*

Although the increased enrollment in colleges and universities has in part been caused by the veterans, it is important to remember that the high enrollment will become a permanent one. To meet this tremendous demand of youth who wish to go to college, the country will be forced to expand present facilities. There are not enough good colleges and universities to go around. It would be relatively easy to say: "We will tighten our admission requirements so that only the few may enter," yet that would be a disservice to the country.

Other recommendations for the improvement of the nation's schools and colleges might easily be enumerated. However, the eighteen listed above appear, on the basis of the survey, to be the most important and should be undertaken as first steps. Obviously, these are long-range proposals. But they can well serve as objectives for communities, states, and the nation. It may take a generation to get them adopted, but no matter how long it takes, educators are convinced that they will be worth while.

It has often been said that civilization faces a race between education and catastrophe. If that be true, then it is more imperative than ever that the United States take the lead in helping education to win the race. As the preamble to the United Nations Educational, Scientific and Cultural Organization (UNESCO) says, "Since wars begin in the minds of men, it is in the minds of men that the defenses of peace must be constructed."

Education has become more important today for the peace of the world than ever before in history. The atomic bomb and the jet plane have made it mandatory that we maintain peace. Education can develop a better understanding among the peoples of the world.

If we can recognize the importance of education on a world-wide scale, we must recognize even more the significance of education for the future welfare and prosperity of our own country. Our public schools, the first line of defense against attacks from within or without, deserve our utmost support. Because our public schools are so important and so necessary for the continuance of our democratic form of government, it is essential that the public extend its support willingly and without reservation. The money that is needed to rebuild the public school system and put it into good working order cannot be invested in any better or more important cause.

Democracy is postulated upon the existence of an educated, intelligent electorate. To make democracy work, it is necessary that we maintain a strong system of free public schools. Nothing less will do.

This is a crusade in which all can enter with enthusiasm and vigor.